Hampshire County Council
www.hants.gov.uk/library
0845 603 5631

08

27. SEP 08.
21. FEB 09.

24. JUN 09.

21. OCT 09

CL.69(02/06.)

...TITL.   FREEMAN

C003876087

D1340237

...is due for return on or before the last date shown
...book not being reserved by
...personal application, post, or
...d details of the book.
...UNTY COUNCIL   100%
...Library   recycled paper

...SHIRE PUBLICATIONS LTD

HAMPSHIRE COUNTY LIBRARY

929.
42

07478 04850

C003876087

SOUTH
DIVISION
FAREHAM
282715

British Library Cataloguing in Publication Data:
    Freeman, J. W. (John William), 1920–
    Surnames. – 3rd ed. – (Discovering; no. 35)
    1. Names, Personal – Great Britain – History
    I. Title
     929.4'2'0941.
    ISBN 0 7478 0485 0.

*Published in 2001 by Shire Publications Ltd, Cromwell House, Church
Street, Princes Risborough, Buckinghamshire HP27 9AA, UK. (Website:
www.shirebooks.co.uk)*
*Copyright © 1968, 1973 and 2001 by J. W. Freeman. First published
1968; reprinted. Second edition 1973; reprinted 1977, 1979, 1983, 1986,
1998 and 1991. Third edition 2001. Number 35 in the Discovering series.
ISBN 0 7478 0485 0.*
*All rights reserved. No part of this publication may be reproduced or
transmitted in any form or by any means, electronic or mechanical,
including photocopy, recording, or any information storage and retrieval
system, without permission in writing from the publishers,*

*Printed in Great Britain by CIT Printing Services Ltd, Press Buildings,
Merlins Bridge, Haverfordwest, Pembrokeshire SA61 1XF.*

Contents

Introduction

Probably the most personal things we possess, and yet take most for granted, are our surnames. We use them daily, occasionally inscribing them with care on important documents, but more often than not scrawling them hurriedly and illegibly on letters and forms. Most of us never give them a second thought. However, a surname is a heritage, passed down from one generation to the next, linking families over the centuries, a bond that unites people throughout the English-speaking world. They are our legacy from the past, our gift to the future.

Every surname is a story in itself. It may tell you where your forebears originated, what their work was, or their social status. It may even tell you the colour of their hair or complexion, if they were bald, or had bandy legs, or were thin or tall, short or fat.

Surnames originated from nicknames, first used by our Anglo-Saxon ancestors. They tacked on nicknames to distinguish one person from others using the same first name. Eric with the mop of flaming hair became Eric the Red, later known as Eric Read, to differentiate him from Eric the Bald, in time to become Eric Ball.

Most surnames fall within one of four groups: nicknames, surnames of occupation or office, local surnames, and surnames of relationship. But within these four groups there is considerable overlapping as British surnames originate from almost every European country and some contain a mixture of two languages or more; a few even originate from Biblical sources or ancient Greece.

While some of our surnames have remained virtually unaltered for centuries, others have been distorted and changed by local dialects and alien tongues and now bear little resemblance to their original spelling or pronunciation. Others were changed by accident or deliberately, by scribes or clerks engaged in compiling official records and tax returns; the changed name was carried forward from one generation to the next and finally adopted as the correct version.

The study of the origins of surnames is no substitute for genealogy and family history. Nevertheless, research connected with the history of surnames can be fun.

In this book I have included briefly the origins of about two thousand surnames. If your name is not mentioned, or you have a very unusual surname, you can conduct your own research into its origins. County archives, with their wealth of ancient documents – wills, tax returns, parish registers – that record family names for centuries, are ideal hunting grounds for tracking down your quarry. If you are patient and search diligently, you may be rewarded. As the old proverb says: 'You had not your name for nothing.'

Nicknames

Nicknames were given for a variety of reasons; a considerable number described the character or disposition of the holder. Many medieval nicknames were cruel and coarse: our ancestors were no respecters of personal feelings; but others clearly reveal the sense of humour they possessed. Many of our ancestors may have tramped through the village either secretly pleased with or inwardly raging at the nickname they had attracted.

If your surname is **Verity** you can be proud of your ancestors; it was taken from the French *vérité*, meaning truth. An early holder of the name was Adam Verite of Worcester, 1275. On the other hand **Gulliver** was coined from the French *goulafre*, meaning glutton. A big eater, William Gulafra was mentioned in the Suffolk division of the Domesday Book of 1086. Was your medieval ancestor the village playboy? Quite probably if your name is **Voisey** or **Vaisey**, taken from the French *envoise*, meaning playful. An early gadabout was Adam le Veyse who lived in Somerset in 1270. Anyone named **Root** has plenty to laugh about. The name originated from Old English *rot*, meaning cheerful. William Root was a freeman of the city of York in 1644. Do not be alarmed if your name is **Daft**. It could mean what it says, but it may have started out as Old English *gedaefte*, meaning gentle or meek. Robert Daft lived in Nottingham in 1230. Good at settling arguments? Could be if your name is **Makepeace** or **Makejoy**. That was the reason the first holders were given the nickname. Gregory Makepais was a freeman of Leicester in 1219. Those who strode about arrogantly soon acquired the nickname *prud,* meaning arrogant. This led to the surnames of **Proud** and later **Prout**. Shropshire had a Richard Prude in 1185. Thomas Lawtye of Yorkshire, 1613, was given his name from Old French *leauté*, meaning loyalty; the modern version of the surname is **Lawtey**.

Refined medieval peasants must have been few and far between but judging from the number of people bearing the surnames **Gentle** and **Hendy** there must have been a few. Old English *gentil* described one who was refined; late English *hendy* meant the same thing. William Hendy lived in Surrey in 1198, while Robert le Gent (the first gentleman?) resided in Hampshire in 1195. Then we have the characters who always seem to take the knocks. Robert le Meke, freeman of York in 1300, was one of the early ones. Today the name still lives on in **Humble** and **Meek**. Those who carried on regardless of everything attracted the nickname *prouz*, meaning valiant, which lives on as **Prowse**. One of the first holders of the name was Richard le Prouz of Hertfordshire, 1207. Possibly a man to be avoided was Godard Grim who lived in Norfolk in 1170. His nickname came from Old English *grim*, meaning fierce. No doubt the modern holders of the surname **Grimm** have softened down somewhat through the centuries.

Do you save your pennies? Maybe not, but if your surname is **Pennefather** your ancestors acquired the nickname from *penig faeda,* Old English for a miser. Among the first careful ones was Robert Panyfade who lived in Sussex in 1296. Are you forgetful? Maybe not, but if you are a **Musard** then your ancestors were absent-minded. The nickname came from the French *musard*, meaning absent-minded or lazy. Perhaps Alfricus Musard of Norfolk, 1134, was always leaving his rake or hoe about. One could imagine the ancestors of someone with a surname like **Sturdy** as big strapping chaps, but the nickname was given to a man of reckless or impetuous nature. What scrapes did Hugo Sturdy get up to in York in 1219? Walter le Orpede who lived in Berkshire in 1255 was no doubt always trying to accomplish the impossible, judging from his nickname, meaning stout-hearted. The name is still with us now, spelt **Orped**. One of the few surnames that has remained unchanged for many centuries is that of **Snell**. Edwinus Snell who lived in Norfolk in 1195 obtained his name from the nickname *snel*, meaning bold or smart.

Two surnames, **Gain** and **Ingham**, though spelt differently, have in fact the same beginnings. They both evolved from the nickname *engaigne,* Old French for trickery. Among early holders of the name with a possible reputation for sharp practice were John le Gayne, who lived in Wakefield in 1275, and Richard Ingaine, a resident of Northumberland in 1130. As a complete contrast we have **Godsall** and **Goodsell**, from 'good soul', a description given to an honest peasant. Ralph Godsoule who lived in Yorkshire in 1219 very probably enjoyed an enviable reputation for honest dealings.

Robert le Quic of Cornwall, 1279, obtained his nickname from the Old English *cwic*, meaning lively or nimble; the modern surname of **Quick** remains virtually unchanged. Anglo-Saxons enjoyed people with a sense of humour. There is no argument why Gilbert le Mirie acquired his nickname in Leicester in 1200; it was taken from Old English *myrige.* Today we know the surname as **Merry**. This nickname was extended slightly to describe a blithe person. Robert Muriweder lived in Bedfordshire in 1214; the name today is **Merryweather**. Always first away at the traffic lights? Could be if your name is **Smart**. It was taken from Old English *smeart*, meaning active. Among early records we have William Smert of Worcester, 1274.

It would be difficult to find a surname more descriptive than **Doolittle**. Probably Walter Dolittle who lived in Yorkshire in 1219 was the village idler. On the other hand, Robert Hastie who lived in Warwickshire in 1202 was probably always in a tearing hurry. There are two modern versions of the surname, **Hasty** and **Haste**. John le Slepere who lived in Kent in 1212 may well have been found fast asleep on more than one occasion. The nickname was given to an inactive person; today the surname is known as **Sleeper**.

People with the name **Mudie** or **Moody** can be forgiven if they think their ancestors were of a temperamental nature; in fact the nickname stemmed from Old English *modig*, meaning bold or brave. One of the first families was found in Scotland in 1365 headed by William Mudy.

Some surnames were derived from unknown sources. This applies to **Catt**. We know Margaret Kat who lived in Lancashire in 1202 was given the nickname in connection with the feline world – but why? Was she catty, spiteful or crafty, or did she walk as softly as a cat? The Old English nickname *dolling* meant the dull one and this led to several surnames, among them **Dollmann, Dolling** and **Dowling**. One of the first records of the surname originates from Worcester in 1275 with Peter Dollyng. Peasants who were dull or slow on the uptake soon acquired nicknames; there was Richard Dollard of Colchester, 1329, and Thomas Dumbel who lived in Warwickshire in 1273. Today, their descendants bear the names **Dullard** and **Dumbell**. The surname **Keen**, however, bears little resemblance to its original meaning; Richard le Kene of Oxford, 1297, acquired it from the nickname *cene*, meaning proud or brave. **Wise** stems from Old English *wis,* meaning wisdom; Roger le Wis lived in Sussex in 1203. On the other hand, **Wiseman** was given at times to a magician or a wizard, but sometimes it was applied ironically to a fool.

At first sight it would appear that the surnames **Rawbone** and **Colt** have very little in common; in fact they are closely linked. William Rabayn who lived in Yorkshire in 1301 acquired his name from Old Norman *rabein,* meaning he had legs as speedy as a colt's. Henry le Colt who resided in Somerset in 1227 was given his nickname because he was as lively as a colt. Hugo le Fox of Cornwall, 1297, was as cunning as a fox; the surname **Fox** has remained unchanged for seven hundred years. William Waps who lived in London in the thirteenth century obtained his nickname from Old English *waeps*, meaning a wasp, probably on account of his biting tongue. Today the surname is usually spelt **Waspe**.

Medieval nicknames with the prefix *wild* were very common; in most cases they were used to indicate the village rake or to describe someone with an untamed spirit. These nicknames were given freely and explain the large number of modern surnames such as **Wildblood**, **Wildcat**, **Wilder**, **Wildbore** and **Wildgoose**. They speak for themselves: as wild as a cat, as wild as a boar, or as wild as a goose. The last name probably referred to a man fond of roaming. Henry Wildegos lived in Shropshire in 1201 and William Wyldeblod resided in

Lancashire in 1366. Richard Wildecat lived in Worcester in 1176. It is interesting to note that this nickname was given a new lease of life some eight centuries later when it was used to describe an oil-well prospector.

More nicknames

Many of our modern surnames bear little resemblance to the nicknames that first led to them. In many cases, however, the original nicknames now form part of our language to describe an individual, a trade or occupation, or are used as adjectives to describe some small part of our way of life or social conditions.

The surname **Gape** was first used as a nickname to describe one who was feeble; it was applied to a peasant who stood and watched rather than got on with the job. **Gathercole** had nothing to do with collecting fuel. Medieval doctors used the term *cold* for choler; if one was ill and sickening for choler, the physician would say his patient was gathering cold (choler). But **Gatherer** was derived from Old English *gaderian*, one who gathered or collected money or dues, usually for guild brethren or a trade guild. If your name is **Gabler** you need have no fear that your ancestors were non-stop talkers; the name originated from the French *gabelier* – a tax collector.

Sometimes surnames can give rise to fancy speculations about one's ancestors. For example, **Earl** does not mean that you had a titled ancestor; more likely he was good at winning events in local pageants, where the victor was usually described as an *eorl*. It sounds almost the same, but **Earley** was used to describe one who was manly, derived from Old English *eorlic*, meaning eagle. It seems a far cry from **Fagg** to the modern obsession with pre-packed food, but the name was used to describe a baker who sold clean bread, derived from Old English *facg*. Maybe Peter Clanvagg who lived in Kent in 1317 was the first of our ancestors to sell wrapped bread.

Colley started out as Old English *colis,* meaning coal black, a nickname given to one with a swarthy complexion or jet-black hair. **Conner** came from *cunnere*, Old English for one who examined or inspected, usually ale; the trade of ale conner was highly respected in medieval England. Today to 'con' a place is slang for checking a building before committing a crime. Gambling is no new pastime; our ancestors were fond of a game of chance, usually dice, and any addict soon found himself labelled as **Chance**. It was also given to men who were unlucky, prone to accidents, or whose crops were always failing. **Catchlove** had nothing to do with a medieval lad chasing his sweetheart; the medieval English word for wolf was *love* and the nickname described a wolf hunter. The same goes for **Catchpole**: it was taken from Old Norman *cachepol*, meaning 'chase fowl', and given to a man who collected poultry in default of money. Later the nickname was given to a tax collector and the man who arrested debtors.

What do you make of **Cannon**? It had nothing in common with military weapons, but originated in the Isle of Man from *cannanan*, the man with a white beard. A maker of playing cards? No, not if your ancestor was named **Carden**. It was derived from the French *cardon*, a thistle – a nickname for a man with an obstinate or stubborn nature. **Casbolt**, a medieval term of reproach, described one with a bald head. Both **Bellows** and **Beloe** derive from the nickname 'bellows-mouth' given to one with a lusty voice. The surname **Best** was taken from medieval English *beste*, the beast, given as a nickname for one with a brutal or savage disposition. **Bowgen** originated from a kinder nickname, *Bon Johan* – French for 'Good John'.

Breakspeare was not a clumsy knight but the victor in a tournament who won the contest by breaking his opponent's lance or spear. The English had *duten* to describe a timid man, one who hesitated or was afraid to make a decision. This led to the surnames **Deuters** and **Dewters**. It is interesting to note that the name was recorded in 1191 and not found again until 1671. Perhaps there were few opportunities for peasants to change their minds – at least from a political point of view.

French *dix mars* stood for ten marks, and English *deux* signified two marks (a mark was an English coin used in the Middle Ages). From these phrases stemmed the surnames **Dismore** and **Dimmer**, although why anyone should have been given the unusual nickname in the first place remains a mystery. The same goes for the nickname 'penny-worth', from the French *denree*; maybe that was all the holder was worth, or perhaps he was mean, but whatever the reason it led to the surname **Dare**. The second Tuesday after Easter Sunday was an important term day, when rents were paid and accounts settled. Our ancestors knew it as *Hocedei*; the surname is now **Hockaday**. It was celebrated from the fourteenth century as a festival day and no doubt led to the expression *to hock* or to pawn in order to raise money.

Some people have always found it difficult to get up for work. Lancashire had its 'knockers up' and many of us depend on an alarm clock. It seems our ancestors had the same trouble; the Old English term *hornblawere* described a man charged with the duty of waking workmen by blowing a horn. I do not expect that many folk named either **Hornblow** or **Hornblower** earn their living that way today, but in 1320 William de la Hornblow was paid a penny a week for the job.

Hard was derived from Old Englsih *heard*, given to a man with a severe or harsh nature. **Hare**, from Old English *hara*, was a nickname for a speedy runner; **Heron** was a man with long thin legs; and **Harlock**, from Old English *har* (grey) and *locc* (lock of hair), was a man with grey hair. **Sanctuary** – from the medieval English *seintuarie*, meaning shrine – was a nickname given to a man who at some time had taken refuge in a church. Any fleeing criminal or peasant who could slip inside the church boundary was safe from his pursuers, and woe betide any lord or baron who sent his men inside the boundary. If a peasant feared his master might carry away his animals or household goods, he drove them into the churchyard for safety. And when the countryside was unsafe through marauding bands of robbers or warring barons, peaceful men and their families took refuge in the church. The law of sanctuary was rarely broken.

Gauche started as a nickname for a left-handed man or one who was awkward, while **Gawler** stemmed from Old English *gafol*, meaning tribute or rent interest, a nickname for one who extorted every penny he could. **Ginger** needs no explanation – one with red hair or a fiery temper. **Gleave** and **Gleve** stem from a nickname for a spearman, or the winner of a race in which a spear or lance was set up as a winning post.

Parlour, today, is used as a surname and also to describe a certain type of room. It came from the Anglo-French word for a lawyer and was used as a nickname for a chatterbox, and also for the servant who attended the parlour, originally the conversation and interview room in a monastery.

At first sight it would appear that **Pettifer** described someone who was small, from the French *petit*, but the surname did in fact stem from an entirely different French origin. It came from *pedefer*, iron foot, a nickname given to a cripple or a soldier who had lost a foot. It was a common nickname and may also have been used of one who was clumsy on his feet. **Peak** and **Peek** came from Old English *peac*, describing a stout, thick-set man. **Carbonnell**, Old French *carbon*, or charcoal, was a nickname given to a man with a swarthy complexion or hair as black as coal. **Bream** was the name given to a man with a fierce disposition, while the opposite, **Dainty** or **Denty**, not always a feminine nickname, described someone who was handsome or possessed a pleasant nature.

Damsell was first applied to a maiden of noble birth and later used to describe a page or young squire as peasants regarded the way of life of these young men at court as being effeminate. **Dance** and **Dancer** come from the nickname given to a professional dancer or a leader of a troupe. One such man was Robert de le Daunce who lived in London in 1305 and danced at the royal court. **Merriman** needs no explanation – John Meryman who lived in Gloucester in 1359 was known as 'the merry one'. **Mildmay** on the other hand described a wild lad and was probably given to apprentices who on occasions kicked over the traces.

Trigg was a surname that was first found in Norfolk and Yorkshire, from the Scandinavian *tryggr* – true, trustworthy or faithful; it was probably given in the first case to a servant or retainer. Again from

Yorkshire and Lincolnshire we find **Wake**, given to a man who was alert; later it described a watchman or guardian of a beacon.

Old English *pegen* denoted a thane, a man who became a tenant of land in return for military service. His share of land was called a furlong or, in parts of England where the Danes settled, a *wong.* Today we know the descendants of the part-time farmer and soldier as **Thain**. One stage lower in the social scale was a **Thews**, first a slave, later a bondsman. William Thewe who lived in York in 1190 was a freeman, having obtained his freedom by one of the many ways open to him. For example, a bondsman or villein who lived in a chartered borough for a year and a day became free; some men obtained their freedom by proving in court that their lord and master had no legal hold over them.

'Backwards and forwards like a shuttle' goes the saying and **Shuttle** was the nickname given to an inconsistent or fickle man. **Sprigg** described a small, slender person while **Stick**, from Old English *sticca*, aptly portrayed a tall slender peasant. **Stickells** denoted a man with a rough, bristly chin.

The Anglo-French word *springalde* was used for a military weapon designed to throw missiles. So if your name is **Springall**, it is probable your ancestors were at some time soldiers in charge of such machines. **Caudell** was a thin gruel mixed with wine or ale, and sweetened and spiced, which was fed to the sick and to women in childbirth. The derogatory nickname was given to a peasant unable to hold strong drink and advised by his friends to stick to caudell. William Certayn of London, 1394, was one of the early holders of **Sartin**, given to men who were self-assured or determined; this nickname is linked to the word *certain*.

Those with the surname **Milk** have the choice of two origins. Our ale-swilling peasant ancestors used it as a nickname for anyone who drank milk in preference to something stronger; it was also used to describe a man with snow-white hair. **Moneypenny** was a nickname given to a rich man or, ironically, a poor one. The records fail to reveal whether Richard Manypeny who lived in Somerset in 1229 was rich or poor. From the French nickname *maltalent*, given to a man with unpleasant manners, stemmed the surname **Maitland**. If your name is **Marrow** your ancestors had no connection with the vegetable world; it came from medieval English *marwe*, meaning companion, mate or lover.

Life was harsh and tough for peasants in medieval England, but these hardworking people fostered a community spirit that has somehow been lost down the centuries. In west Berkshire, some of the finest open field farming in the country was practised. Every man cultivated his own strip, but land held in common, especially the meadowland, was farmed by the entire community. From the Teutonic *scipe*, meaning fellowship, sprang the surname **Manship**, probably given to the man who organised the mowing and haymaking for the common meadow.

Law and order were of prime importance in those days. *Laghles* referred to a man who was uncontrolled by the law – a nickname for an outlaw. Today, the surname is simply **Lawless**, and Thomas Lagheles, a freeman of York in 1360, obtained the name from his father, who must have obtained a free pardon for whatever crime he committed. Adam, son of Lagheman, who lived in Lancashire in 1246, took his father's name as a surname, known now as **Lawman**. This official was charged with the duty of declaring the law and seeing it was carried out.

Taken from the Latin *firminus*, **Firmin** was the nickname given to a man with strong or firm convictions, while **Fitton** stemmed from a man notorious for his habit of lying or a reputation for being deceitful. **Daggar** was given to a peasant who carried a dagger (the usual arms were cudgels or staffs). He who walked through the village with his head high and with dignity soon attracted the nickname *dein* – the worthy man, now known as **Dain**.

Barnacle has no connection with the sea; it came from the French *bernac*, a powerful bit for a horse, and was given to a man who tamed wild horses or to an individual with an unrestrained temper. **Bassett** means a man of low stature – today we would refer to him as 'Shorty' – while **Bean** and **Been** were given to men known to be pleasant or genial, though on occasions they were given to a man of few possessions ('not worth a bean'). **Beldam**, from the French *belle dame*, a fine lady, was usually a derogatory nickname, sometimes given to peasant women who tried to emulate their mistresses.

The prefix *fair* led to many surnames: **Fairfax**, one with fair hair; **Fairfoot**, one with a light foot; and **Fairhead**, the nickname for a peasant who possessed a beautiful hood. **Fairman** usually described a blond man (Anglo-Saxons as a rule had fair hair, the Normans dark hair) and **Fairweather** was given to the man blessed with a bright and sunny disposition. The village nagger or scold was known as **Atter**, from Old English *ator*, the one with the biting tongue or the shrew. **Barefoot** was a nickname given to pilgrims or those doing penance; in medieval England thousands made the journey each year to Canterbury and other shrines.

Among the older Anglo-Saxon surnames we find **Kemp** from *cempa*, used to describe a warrior and, later, a wrestler or athlete. The name was recorded as far back as AD 902 with Eadulf Cempa who lived in Worcester. **Knatchbull**, meaning the man who felled the bull, was the nickname given to butchers, and **Langbant** indicated a tall child while **Lank** was given to a tall, slim man.

A man who took something quickly by a trick was known as **Wrench**, but the slippery customer, the lad hard to catch, became **Wrey**. The well-fed, contented-looking peasant was known among his friends as **Wellfitt**, and **Wightman** was the strong or brave man. Some people always seemed to find themselves in trouble: everything they touched went wrong. Today their name has become **Travell**. The 'here today, gone tomorrow' type was just as common, resulting in the surname **Scattergood**. **Preety** was a nickname for a cunning man.

Why should men get such nicknames as 'seven pence'? Wylliam Sevynpenys lived in Suffolk in 1524; goodness only knows why he was tagged with a name like that. The surname has changed somewhat since then, but it is still with us, disguised as **Seppings**. And how about **Shilling**? Did he possess one shilling, did he help to make them, or was it derived from some long-standing village joke? **Sadd** is easy enough – Henry Sadde of Essex, 1229, known as the sad man, while **Samways** was used of a man who was slow on the uptake.

Rump had nothing to do with meat, but was an unkindly nickname given to an ugly, raw-boned hulk of a man. **Rutter** brings back a reminder of a musical instrument long since forgotten: the rote was something similar to a fiddle, and the nickname was given to a musician who played one. The surname could also have been derived from *rotier,* a French word meaning highwayman or ruffian.

There are a considerable number of surnames that were derived from oath words or sayings. One in particular is **Godsave** from *Godes half*, a frequent saying meaning in God's name. This must have been a very common expression in London, judging by the number of families that inherited this surname. Another saying was 'Go lightly', used both as an instruction and a nickname for messengers, resulting in the surname **Golightly**. The direct opposite applied to **Ambler** or **Amblene**, given to one with a slow walk or ambling gait. **April** and **Avrill** were derived from the nickname given to one as fickle or changeable as the month of April, and sometimes to a person who always seemed full of the joys of spring.

Lightburn had two origins, each the exact opposite of the other. It was used as a nickname to describe someone as active as a small child and also for one known to be gentle and mild. **Lightbody** was similar, given to one with a small or light body and to an active and gay individual. A man with a light, springy step or fleet of foot was soon known as **Lightfoot**; the nickname was also given to messengers. A lazy person or rustic fool resulted in **Chubb**, a prominent chin or long beard gave us **Chinn**. A cub or kitten, or the young of any beast, was known as a *chitte* and this led to the surname **Chittock**.

Old English *healf cniht* meant a half knight, one who held land by paying half the cost towards a knight or armed horseman in his lord's army for forty days, and at times was used as a derogatory expression to describe a knight with very little skill. This ancient term lives on in **Halfknight**.

Anglo-Saxons were very conscious of their civic duties. **Portman** comes from the word for a townsman, one of the body of citizens chosen to administer the affairs of a borough (councillors). **Revel** was not given to a pleasure seeker, but to a man known to rebel against authority, or one with excessive pride. A **Ripper** was not a man bent on destruction, but the nickname for a maker or seller of baskets. The term was also used for the men who brought the fish to sell in London.

Papillion was derived from the Latin *papilio*, a butterfly, the nickname that aptly described a man who was inconsistent or imprudent, possibly flitting from one trade or scheme to another without thought or reason. **Parent** may at times have started as a surname of relationship, but generally was used of a man with a fine figure. **Old** did not denote one who was venerable but distinguished father from son, or the eldest brother from the rest.

From the French *orgueil*, meaning pride, stems the surname **Orgel**; Gerard Orgul who lived in London in 1305 was known as 'the proud one'. **Arlott** referred to a young lad or a vagabond or rogue, while **Allmark** and **Almack** were nicknames for one who refused to pay more than half a mark for his purchases.

All through the Middle Ages pilgrims made the long and dangerous journey to Rome or even the Holy Land. On the return journey they carried a palm branch as a sign that they had indeed completed the pilgrimage. Today we know the nickname as **Palmer**, given to distinguish them from those who made pilgrimages to nearer places like Canterbury.

The Old English personal name *Godric* signified good ruler and was used as a nickname for those who used their power wisely. First mentioned in the Domesday Book, a later record was that of Gaufridus filius Godrici, resident in Berkshire in 1207. Goodrich Castle in Hereford was 'Godric's castle'. Today there are at least nine variations of the surname, including **Goodrich**, **Goodwright** and **Gooderidge**.

Characteristically, the Anglo-Saxons had a nickname for one who was slow on the uptake. *Finc* described someone who was a simpleton, or as stupid as a bird. This stigma did not apply to the family headed by Santic Fink who resided in the City of London in 1231 and which was prosperous enough to give its name to Finch Lane. Today's descendants bear the surname **Finch** or **Vink**.

Another uncomplimentary nickname was that acquired from Old English *martre*, meaning weasel. From this jibe has evolved the surnames **Marter** and **Martyr**. William Martre resided in Hampshire in 1148.

For centuries the curse of the plague troubled England and no one, rich or poor, was safe from the terrible disease. Those who survived were often left with facial scars and were referred to as having 'God's mark'. This unfortunate nickname has remained unchanged to this day as **Godsmark**. The Old German *Hugibert*, meaning bright mind, was given as a nickname to one with a bright, alert mind. One such citizen was Roger Hubert, a native of Northumberland in 1199. The name is unchanged, spelt **Hubert** or **Hubbard**.

Judging from some of the nicknames bestowed on village folk, there must have been an astonishing variety of residents even in one small village. Old English *Aelfhean*, meaning 'elf high', was probably given to one of short stature. Today's surnames are **Elphick** and **Alphege**. Old English *Aelfric*, meaning 'elf ruler', led to the surnames **Aldrich**, **Eldridge** or **Elrick**. Another not so complimentary nickname was *Eoforheard*, meaning boar's head. Over the centuries it has changed to **Everitt** and **Everard**. Old English *trik* described a cheater or deceiver, a nickname given to one of dubious business principles. Adam Le Tricur resided in Wakefield in 1275, by which time the surname had become respectable. It is now spelt **Tricker** or **Trickett**.

Peacocc was a nickname given to someone as proud as a peacock, then later became a personal name, and later a surname. From Richard Pocok of Somerset, 1225, we have progressed to **Peacock** and **Pocock**. The nickname *Cointerel* originated from the French for a fop or beau, although it is hard to imagine how any poor peasant could have acquired such a nickname. Do those named **Quantrell** or **Quintrell** realise that their ancestors were the best dressed folk in the village?

Old English *Gal* described one who was merry or bubbly, probably the life and soul of the village. Perhaps Alicia Gale who lived in Huntingdon in 1202 possessed these qualities. The surname has remained virtually unchanged as **Gale**, with **Gayle** as an alternative.

The verb *to loll* stems from medieval English *lolle*, to droop, dangle or lean idly. Perhaps Robert Lolliere who resided in Huntingdon in 1160 used to hang about on village street corners. The surname today is **Loller**.

The Normans had the nickname *Testard*, meaning big head, an uncomplimentary title to describe the physical or mental attributes of the holder. It was a common surname in Sussex and today it is written as **Tester**. A name that has remained unchanged for over eight hundred years is **Sage**, derived from Old French *sage*, meaning wise. One of the first holders of the surname was Robert Le Sage who lived in Shropshire in 1185.

Everyone has heard the expression Jack the lad. At first, *lad* described one of low birth or a servant; later, it described one of low morals. Little changed, the surname is now **Ladd**. The surname

Armstrong speaks for itself, meaning strong in the arm. Well known in the border counties, William Armstrang was a citizen of Carlisle in 1250.

Grant and **Grand** stem from the French nickname *Grand*, meaning tall. Today, the nickname would probably be 'Lofty'. No doubt Wilfin Graunt, residing in Suffolk in 1150, was head and shoulders above his fellow villagers. **Thick** was a physical not a mental description, taken from medieval English *thikke*, meaning thick or stout. The nickname *Krok*, denoting something crooked or a hook, described a sly or cunning person. Matthew Croc was mentioned in the Hampshire Pipe Rolls for 1158 when the name must already have become respectable. Passed down over the centuries, the surname is now **Krook** or **Crook**.

The Anglo-Saxons knew a young sheep as a *tegga*. It was soon used as a nickname, probably for one who was either stupid or frisky, depending on their personality. This led to the surnames **Tegg** and **Tigg**. John de Goly, a citizen of Worcester in 1275, was no doubt the village clown or jester. The nickname stemmed from Old French *joli* and was given to someone who was lively or full of spirit. The surname lives on as **Jolliff** or **Jolley**.

Bridd was Old Englsih for bird; as a nickname it could have been given to one who was as timid as a bird, or hopped about like one. Perhaps those named **Bird**, **Byrd** or **Bride** today are as light on their feet. On the other hand, William le Hardy, residing in Berkshire in 1220, acquired his nickname from Old French *hardi*, describing a bold or fearless person. The name is now **Hardy** or **Hardie**.

A considerable number of nicknames that became personal names had military associations. Both **Osman** and **Osmond** originate from Old English *Osmund*, meaning God's protector. **Ironsides** is self-explanatory, a term given to those valiant in battle. The most famous holder of this name was Edmond Ironside, mentioned in Anglo-Saxon records in 1057. Teutonic *Hildeberht* or French *Ilbert* were nicknames meaning 'battle glorious'. Walter Ilbert was a citizen of York in 1230, probably living a peaceful, non-military life. In telephone books today we see the names as **Ilbert**, **Hibbard** and **Hilbert**.

The nickname *Hervé*, meaning 'battle worthy', was introduced at the time of the Norman invasion. Willelmus Hervici resided in Norfolk in 1242, a favourite county for the Bretons. Fortunately there is now no need for those named **Harvey** or **Hervey** to buckle on their two-handed sword.

The French nickname *Maugier* meant 'council spear'; it became a personal name. One of the early holders was Malger who came to England at the time of the Battle of Hastings and was given lands at Tolleshunt in Essex, which was then named Tolleshunt Major. There are two modern variations of the surname: **Major** and **Mauger**.

Mentioned in the Domesday Book, *Edmundos* acquired his name from the nickname *Eadmund*, 'prosperity protector'. Today, his descendants are known as **Edmunds** or **Edmond**.

Without a doubt **Shakespeare** must be one of the most celebrated surnames in the English language. The nickname was given to a spearman, or man at arms. Simon Shakespeare who lived in Somerset in 1324 had no idea how famous one of his descendants would become.

The origins of some nicknames have vanished centuries ago, even though the subsequent surnames have remained unchanged for seven hundred years. Old English *Osbern* is translated as 'God bear', though what it meant is uncertain. Walter Osborn resided in Cornwall in 1310. There are now three variations of the name: **Osborn**, **Usborne** and **Hosburn**.

Old English *god* became *good*, and *wine* meant friend, so *Godwine*, meaning good friend, became a popular first name and later surname. Two variations remain to this day, **Godwin** and **Goodwin**.

The nickname *Jackdaw* (not very complimentary) became **Dawes** or **Daw**. It is interesting to note that Lovekin Dawes, a citizen of Oxford in 1279, had a first name that also became a surname. *Lovekin* meant 'little love', an endearing pet name. There are at least nine modern spellings of this surname, including **Lovekin**, **Luckin** and **Lukyn**.

Personal appearances were always seized on as excuses for nicknames. *Dunn* was Old English for dull or brown, and was often given to a man who was dark or swarthy. John le Dunn was a Hertfordshire citizen in 1198. The name today is still **Dunn** or **Donne**.

Doughty and **Dufty** originated from Old English *dohtig*, meaning valiant or strong. The Normans had a nickname *Dru*, meaning sturdy, which was no doubt bestowed on a well-set peasant. It has changed little: today we know it as **Drew**.

Alexander has been a first name and surname for centuries. It originated from a Greek word meaning 'defender of men'. Thomas Alexander was mentioned in the Suffolk Subsidy Rolls for 1283. **Shad** is a strange surname with an unusual origin. The Anglo-Saxons had a fish they called a shad, from *sceado*. Why such a nickname should be given has been lost centuries ago. Old English *cyning* has become King. It was a nickname given to one with a regal bearing or one who acted as king in a play or pageant. William King, resident in Huntingdon in 1259, may have taken part in a pageant or religious play. His descendants' names remain unchanged as **King** or **Kinge**. Still on the subject of royalty, we have the surnames **Kenward** and **Kennard** which stem from *cyneweard*, the royal guardian.

Isabella Virgo, resident in Warwick in 1428, probably received her name through playing the part of the Virgin Mary in a miracle play.

Her name is still the same today, **Virgo**, or **Vergine** and **Virgin**.

There is little doubt as to the origins of **Roughead** or **Ruffhead**. It described one with rough shaggy hair. **Sarson** was taken from the French *Sarrazin*, meaning Saracen, a nickname for one with a swarthy complexion.

One surname with at least thirteen variations is **Ewen**, **Ewan** or **Ewings**. It has a complicated history, coming first from the Greek for wellborn, which was later translated into the Gaelic and Irish languages. The Welsh called it *Ougein*. It became a very popular first name, then a surname. It travelled from Wales into Scotland. The Bretons introduced the name into East Anglia. Walter Ywain, an early holder of the name, lived in Warwick in 1202. The first name *Tew* also found its way from Wales into England; it meant fat or plump. Hugh le Tyn lived in Chester in 1286. The name has changed little since then, now spelt **Tew**. Also originating from Wales was the personal name *Gwenhwyvar*, meaning, fair, white or smooth. Living in Shropshire not far from the Welsh border in 1296 was Mabilia Jeneur. The name is known today as **Jennifer** or **Juniper**.

Another female pet name or nickname was Old French *dous*, meaning sweet or pleasant. It was later taken as a man's surname. Godfrey Le Douz was mentioned in Sussex records in 1296. **Dowse** or **Duce** are today's versions of the name.

Every age had its favourite form of greeting. In medieval England a favourite saying was 'I hope to have a good year'. This led to a nickname, probably given to one who was fond of the saying. Then it became the surname **Goodyear** or **Goodier**.

People with dark hair or complexions attracted many nicknames. The surnames **Cole** and **Coales** originated from Old English *col*, meaning black, which described a person who was dark-skinned or swarthy. **Corbett** stems from Old French *corbet*, a raven. This nickname was given to someone with dark features.

Old English *cynebeald*, literally 'kin-bold', was perhaps used as a nickname for someone who was very proud of his family. Richard Cemble was a citizen of Huntingdon in 1185; his descendants became either **Kemble** or **Kimball**. **Durrant** or **Dorran** originated from the French *durant*, meaning obstinate. Was John Durant, resident in Surrey in 1222, the odd man out in his village? Both **Eagle** and **Eagell** are self-explanatory, possibly originating from the bird of prey of that name. Why people attracted this nickname remains a mystery. Did they have a hooked nose or sharp features? Or did it apply to their nature or even to their predatory behaviour?

Abbot and **Labbet** are not occupational surnames (abbots were celibate and had no one to inherit their names). The nickname arose from a person who conducted himself like a man of the church.

Cardinal was a nickname given to a man who dressed in red or acted like a cardinal. Contrary to popular belief **Isaac** or **Islake** are not necessarily Jewish surnames; the medieval surname was certainly not Jewish. It was taken from the Hebrew *Issac*, meaning laugh. It was first recorded in the Domesday Book, which suggests it was Norman in its original form. Willelmus filius Ysac who lived in Essex in 1206 took his father's first name as his own surname.

If your surname is **Tooth** it does not signify that your ancestors were medieval dentists. It was the nickname given to one with prominent teeth. No doubt Robert Tothe, a citizen of York in 1219, had that sort of mouth.

Old French *pecke* and Latin *peccatum*, both meaning sin, led to a curious nickname. What misdeeds did this unfortunate jibe refer to? What village gossip led to this odious label being thrust on one of the villagers? Today's families of **Petch** or **Peachey** should not have any misgivings about their ancestors. Possibly their only sin was to miss church one Sunday.

Old English *readi* was a nickname given to a citizen who was always in a state of preparation – against what, alas, we do not know now – but it was probably given to one who was quick, ready or prompt. It led to today's surnames of **Ready**, **Readey** or **Reddie**. There is little doubt about the origins of **Nightingale**. It stemmed from Old English *Nihtegale*, a common nickname for one with a sweet or melodious voice. Richard Nightingale, resident in Bedfordshire in 1227, inherited his name from his mother, the village soprano.

Occupational surnames

Occupational surnames arose from the practice of quoting a man's trade followed by his forename. Occasionally a man would be given a trade name as a nickname, especially if his trade or occupation was an unusual one. The study of medieval occupational surnames has revealed the remarkable variety and specialist nature of the trades and professions of our ancestors. Although many of these occupations disappeared centuries ago they still live on in our modern surnames. Monks, priors and abbots took vows of celibacy and could not found families, so the surnames referring to such people were nicknames given to men who either aped these church officials or worked for them.

The Anglo-French word *canceler* described a court usher, custodian of records or a secretary. Reinbald Cancelor was mentioned in the Domesday Book. Today, the name is used both as a surname and as a state title – **Chancellor**. Medieval royalty or nobility were forced to carry out extended tours of their domains and the chamberlain, the official responsible for organising the private chambers during their travels, was an important man. Present holders of the surname **Chamberlain** must be proud to know that their name has remained unchanged for over seven centuries. Another important household official was the steward, coined from Old English *stigweard*. The name first described an official of the royal household, then later the steward of the manor. Today, we know the name as **Steward** or **Stuart**, one of the first being Reginald le Stiward of Dorset, 1205. **Monk** does not signify an ancestor who was a monk, but rather a man who worked for monks, taken from Old English *munuc*. William Munc of Essex, 1222, did work at a monastery. Later the name was used as a nickname.

One of our oldest local officials is a reeve; in Anglo-Saxon times he acted as a constable, and later as a magistrate. The nickname was taken from Old English *refa*; today we know it as **Reeve** or **Reeves**. Richard del Reves of Lancashire was a local official in 1332. Anyone with the name of **Sargent** can be proud of the wealth and tradition behind the surname. At first it applied to a general servant, then a court official, and after that a tenant under the rank of knight, which led to the rank of sergeant in the army, the rank immediately below that of officer. Another ancient office is that of constable. It was taken from the Latin *comes stabuli*, and from it stems the surname **Constable**. Originally it described an officer of the stables, then a governor of a fortress and finally, in about 1328, a parish constable. Among early holders of the name we find Richard Conestabl of Cornwall, 1130.

Richard Cartwrytte lived in Cheshire in 1290. His nickname was derived from *craet-wyrhta*, meaning a maker of carts. There may be a few **Cartwrights** engaged in the manufacture of motor cars, but probably very few make carts. If your name is **Pavier** or **Paver**, then your ancestors were engaged in a trade that still exists today – laying pavements. William le Pavour lived in London in 1281. The surname **Writer** speaks for itself; it originally described a copier of manu-scripts. The writers formed a guild in London in 1422, but the first record of the name comes from Worcestershire with Adam le Wrytar in 1275. A vastly different trade was followed by the ancestors of anyone named **Thrower**. A thread thrower was a man who converted raw silk into silk thread. Thomas le Throwere followed his trade in Essex in 1326. Another surname that owes its beginnings to domestic service is that of **Hall**. It was derived from Old English *heall* and was given to a worker or servant at the hall, the old name for the manor house. Warin de Halla carried out his duties in Essex in 1178.

English medieval craftsmen were among the finest in Europe and although some of the skills and trades have been lost we still have their surnames to remind us of them. It may be one of our commonest names, but **Smith** has an uncommon history behind it. Linked with this surname is **Smither**, **Smithers** and **Smyth**, not to forget a further twelve varieties. The name stemmed from Old English *smid*, meaning a blacksmith or farrier. It is one of the few surnames recorded before the Norman invasion; we know of an Ecceard Smid who lived in AD 975. A later version was the surname of John Smythiere who resided in Warwickshire in 1379. In medieval England every village and hamlet had its own smith; this accounts for the profusion of the surname. A French word *tornour* described a skilled man who fashioned objects of wood, metal or bone on a lathe. These men were soon called turners, leading to the surname **Turner**. It became a common surname due to the number of craftsmen engaged in this work. Warner le Turnur of London, 1180, was one of the early ones.

A Saxon *waegnwyrhta* was a wagon builder or **Wainwright**. **Furner** was French for a baker; his companion **Whitbread** was the man who baked or sold white bread, considered a luxury as it was made from wheat. **Capers** was the man who made capes, while the cap maker was known as **Capper**. Both **Yeoman** and **Yeamen** were servants or attendants in a noble house; they ranked between the squire and the page – the first of the middle class. Cinnamon was in great demand as a spice; the trader who sold it was known as **Cannell**.

Thomas **Coney**, a freeman of York in 1323, was a dealer in rabbit skins, and a man who made nails was known as **Clower**. Still used as both a surname and a tradename, **Cutler** was first recorded in London. **Clapper** had a double meaning: it was used as a nickname for a man who lived near the clapper bridge; it also described a chatterbox, hence today's 'claptrap'. **Elliman** and **Ellerman** sold oil, mainly for lamps, to our medieval ancestors. **Gatward** was the goat keeper. **Gater** lived near the city gate and **Gaunter** either made or sold gloves.

Richard le **Batt**, who lived in Sussex in 1296, acquired his nickname from his trade of making cudgels, known as *batts*. (In 1575 the word *bat* in reference to a game was introduced in Sussex, and since then the game of cricket has never looked back.) **Last** originated from the man who made the wooden mould of the foot for a shoemaker. Richard Last who lived in Suffolk in 1385 was a shoemaker and probably made his own lasts.

The French word for farrier was *maréschal*, from which originated the surnames **Marshall** and **Maskell**. The name was later also given to a high officer of the state. Whether Henry le Marscal who lived in Somerset in 1238 was concerned with politics or horses is no longer known. Some people are blessed with rare or unusual occupational surnames such as **Jester** and **Juggler**. John Gestour of Colchester, 1377, acquired his nickname from the French *geste*, meaning a mimic or professional reciter of romances, while William le Gugelour who lived in Somerset in 1250 owed his nickname to the fact that he was a juggler. Other surnames deriving from medieval entertainers include **Tredgett**, **Tredjitt** and **Trudgett** from the medieval English *trigit*, meaning to juggle or deceive. We have a record of a Richard Tridgitt who lived in Suffolk in 1674; he may have come from a family of magicians.

Richard le Pickere resided in Yorkshire in 1188 and Nicholas Pike was a Cornishman mentioned in 1344. Both families owe their name to their occupation of making pickaxes. Today the names are spelt **Picker** and **Pike**. Probably the Cornish branch of the family made pickaxes for the tin mines.

Judging by the number of occupational surnames connected with food, our ancestors must have been fond of eating. **Kew** originated from the French *cu* – to do with cooking, first mentioned in Norfolk in 1196 with Roger le Cu. The old English version was *coc*, now known as **Cook**. One of the few Old English surnames, it was first recorded in AD 950 with Aelfsige Coc. Both these names referred rather to a seller of cooked meats than to a man who actually cooked them. Our ancestors were not slow to praise or condemn, and any man who sold first-class ale soon enjoyed a reputation that attracted the nickname 'good ale'. Today, the descendants of these brewers or sellers of fine ale bear the surnames **Goodall** or **Goodale**. Among the early families we find William Godale who sold his ale in Bedfordshire in 1244. **Cater** owes its origins to the term given to someone who purchased provisions on a large scale, usually for a manor or other large dwelling place; an early big spender was Elias le Catur who lived in Cornwall in 1271.

The surnames **Judge** and **Judges** speak for themselves, taken from Old French *juge,* meaning a law official. Thomas Judges, who lived in Suffolk in 1524, may have come from a legal family, but the large number of these surnames suggests that the name may have been given as a nickname. Early medieval England depended mainly on the bow for its defence and many occupational surnames are connected with this weapon. **Arrowsmith**, **Arsmith** and **Harismith** all derive from a smith who made arrow heads; William le Arweesmyth lived in Essex in 1324. **Alabaster** originates from Old French *Arbalestier,* meaning crossbowman. Ralph Alebaster of Essex, 1200, was probably a professional soldier. Another surname that in its early days may have been connected with the making of arrows was **Setter**. Later it was given to building workers who set bricks or stone. It was a common London surname; among early records we find Roger le Stere who resided in the City in 1278. The bellfounder was an important medieval craftsman; the Normans called him a *saintier.* This led to the surnames **Senter**, **Sainter** and **Santer**. The name was more common in large towns and cathedral cities; the city of York had a Roger Santer in 1333.

Today, engineers are employed in hundreds of trades, and the family surname of **Jenner** has played no small part in this achievement. The French dubbed the maker of military machines with the nickname *Engineor.* In time this was given to any engineer, civil or military. This surname was more common in London in medieval times; we find Robert le Ginnur in the City of London records for 1229. Wood was the main source of heat and power in medieval England. Men were employed in burning ashes to make potash. The Normans had a nickname for these men – *brenna,* meaning to burn. Thomas Asborner lived in Sussex in 1332; no doubt he made a good living working in the rich Sussex forests. Today the surname lives on as **Ashburn** or **Ashburner**.

Probably a local hardworking tradesman acquired the nickname **Beaver**, while **Barley** was the maker or seller of barley bread or cakes. The **Barber** was more than a man who cut hair; he also dabbled in surgery and dentistry. Old English *Bendan*, bend the bow, became **Bender**, the man who made bows, and **Cakebread** the baker who made bread in the form of flattened cakes.

If your surname is **Fidler** or **Vidler**, have no fears. Your ancestors were not medieval conmen but were men who played the fiddle for hire, usually as travelling entertainers. John Fydeler lived in York in 1380. If you are a **Barker** then you have the choice of two occupations among your ancestors. John le Bercher of Hampshire, 1212, acquired his name from the French *berchier*, meaning shepherd, while Jordan le Barkere who resided in Essex in 1255 got his name from Old English *bark*, meaning to tan. **Barkhouse**, however, has only one meaning – someone who worked in a tannery. One such man was Thomas de Barkhous, a tannery worker who lived in Yorkshire in 1379.

The ancestors of **Kidgell** or **Kiggel** were engaged in the manufacture or selling of a lethal weapon. The Old English for a cudgel was *cycgel* and this nickname was given to men who made or sold cudgels. Godwin Kiggel who lived in Suffolk in 1221 must have been indirectly responsible for a large number of broken heads. Centuries ago it was common practice for men to carry personal weapons. One entrepreneur was Aeluric Chebbel who carried on his trade in Bury St Edmunds in 1095. The name has been handed down the generations and today we know it as **Keeble** or **Kibble**.

Even in medieval England many people were engaged in trades connected with women's fashions. Some of these occupations are still with us, others have vanished over the centuries. Agnes le Ceintere who lived in Worcestershire in 1275 acquired her name from the French *ceinture*, waist belt; she was in fact a maker of these waist belts. The surname is not so common today, but there are still a few people about who have the name **Center**. Bartholomew le Camisur was a London tradesman who resided in the City in 1282. His name originated from Old Norman *camise* or *chemise*, meaning shirt. He was a manufacturer of this garment, which in those days was worn by both men and women. The modern surnames are **Camis**, **Camoys** or **Keemish**. Those with the name **Draper** or **Drapper** can reckon that their forebears were at the other end of the line, selling these goods. Hugo Drapier who lived in Hampshire in 1148 was one of the first Englishmen to follow this trade. At first, drapers sold or made only woollen cloth; the sale of garments came later. Robert le Dressour of Lancashire, 1324, was a 'dresser' of fabrics: he gave them a smooth finish. Today the surname lives on as **Dresser**, though it is believed that the name was later acquired through arranging textile displays. William le Fulur of Warwickshire, 1221, Baldwin Tuckere of Sussex, 1236, and Robert le Walker of Yorkshire, 1260, had one thing in common: they all worked in the textile trade. A tucker or fuller was a man who thickened cloth by beating it in water; a walker was a man who effected the same result by treading the cloth. The names live on as **Fuller**, **Tucker** and **Walker**.

There is an old saying, 'a chip off the old block'. There are many surnames to which this could apply. The names **Chapman**, **Chipping** or **Chipchase**, and **Chapper**, **Cheapen** or **Chipper** all owe their origin to either Old English *ceapmann*, a merchant trader, or *ceapian*, a man who traded cheap goods. These were nearly always travelling traders who went to country fairs and towns on market days, or who travelled the countryside, knocking on the doors of cottages and manors alike, and they were usually made welcome, especially by the women folk. Henry le Chipman lived in Hampshire in 1327 (when he was home) and John Chaper of Surrey was mentioned in county records in 1200.

Without money, the journeys of these travelling traders would have been in vain. Medieval England possessed one of the finest coinage systems in Europe. About thirty mints were in operation up and down the country, and many families owe their surnames to ancestors engaged in this industry. The hammer-man was the craftsman who beat out the coins on an anvil; John le Hammer of Sussex, 1332, was such a man. His craft is remembered in the modern surname of **Hammerman**. Today's surname **Minter** owes its origins to the same source, and William le Myntere who resided in Warwickshire in 1221 acquired his name from old English *myntere*, meaning a moneyer. A besant was a gold coin issued in England during the Middle Ages; the minting of this coin led surnames such as **Besant**, **Besent**, **Bessent** and **Bezant**. Lefwin Besant was employed at a mint in London in 1147. Not far away the first bankers and money lenders were already in operation. William Lumbart resided in the City in 1200; the reason for his nickname was that the first bankers and money lenders came from Lombardy. We have not only the surnames of **Lombard** and **Lumbard** to remind us of those early financial wizards, but also Lombard Street in the City of London, where they first set up in business.

Perhaps you can guess the origin of **Ackerman**, derived from Old English *aecermann*, meaning farmer. An early son of the soil with this name was Robert le Akerman who lived in Essex in 1223. But what about the name **Farmer**? Strange as it seems, the name was taken from the Latin *firmarius*, meaning tax collector. William le Fermer of Essex, 1238, was one of the early ones. It was only later, when the farmer collected rents for his lord's lands, that the term applied to a man engaged in agricultural work. Two names alike in their spelling but with entirely different origins are **Harbisher** and **Habbeshaw**. The first named was taken from the French *herbege*, meaning host, given to someone who kept a lodging house. One medieval innkeeper was Thomas le Harbegur in Sussex in 1198. Reginald le Hauberger was a maker of *hauberks* or coats of mail in London in the thirteenth century and gave the surname of Habbeshaw to his descendants.

The surname **Pannier** was first given to a man who made pans, then to a hawker who used baskets slung over a mule 'pannier fashion'. John le Panner lived in Essex in 1262 but we do not know if he made pans or earned his living as a hawker using baskets. But if your name is **Pannell** your ancestors made panels, a term which applied to many types, from panels used in housing to panels that were part of horse saddles.

One of the oldest British occupations is that of dispensing hospitality. In early medieval times the monasteries were the main centres of food and lodging for travellers. The French *hostelier* described one who received or entertained guests, especially in a monastery. The name later came to describe a keeper of a hostelry or inn and later still a stableman. Robert le Hostler resided in Norfolk in 1275. Now we know the surnames as **Ostler**, **Hosteller** and **Hustler**. The Old English word *inn-mann* has become **Inman** today. William Inman kept an inn in York in 1379.

Many men laboured in the quarries, extracting stone, chalk, sand and flint. William atte Quarere worked in Sussex in 1332. Today his descendants named **Quarry** and **Quarrie** are scattered all over the country.

A more genteel occupation, often carried out by women, was that of making long cloaks or capes. Walter Cape, resident in Kent in 1190, and Maud Cape, a London citizen in 1275, were themselves connected with this trade or their families were. The modern spelling is **Cape** or **Cope**.

Many men worked for the king. One of the monarch's favourite pastimes was hunting, and the upkeep of the royal forests was an important task. The man who tended the herds of deer and protected them from poachers was given the nickname *hurt* or *hart*. This is one of the rare surnames which predate the Norman Conquest, proving that hunting was popular with Anglo-Saxon kings. Aelfric Hort resided in Hampshire in 1060, probably working in the New Forest. There are several variations of the surname today, including **Hart**, **Hurt** or **Hort**.

An occupation that has remained with us down the centuries is that of collecting or manufacturing salt. Old English *sealtere* described a maker or seller of salt. Philip le Salter, a resident of Somerset, was no doubt engaged in this trade. Seasalter in Kent acquired its name as early as AD 858 as the salt house or salt works on the sea. It is possible that some of the first surnames came from this area. Now the names are **Salter**, **Saulter** or **Sawter**.

Ever since ale has been brewed there has been a need for casks. The man who made or repaired wooden casks, buckets or tubs was known as a *couper*. Robert le Cupere plied his trade in Surrey in 1176. Today's versions are **Cooper** and **Copper**.

At first sight the surname **Stew** might suggest something culinary, but nothing could be further from the truth. The name originated from *stewe,* a fish pond, and the name was given to the man who looked after it. One such man was William Steweman, recorded in the Suffolk Subsidy Rolls for 1327.

Long before any Frenchman wheeled through England with onions strapped to his bicycle his ancestors had already done a similar thing, but probably on foot or with a packhorse or mule. The surnames **Onion** and **Onyon** are derived from the Norman *oignon*, describing an onion seller. One of the early purveyors of this versatile vegetable was Robert Onnyon who plied his trade in Suffolk in 1568.

A fitch was a pointed iron instrument, not unlike a spear or lance, which was used as both a military weapon and a civilian tool. The name stems from Old French *fiche* and was given to the workmen who made them for military use or who used them as tools. John le Figg resided in Sussex in 1327, no doubt employed in the Sussex iron works. His descendants are known as **Figs** and **Fitch**.

Rusher derived from the man who cut or sold rushes, which were used for many reasons in medieval times, especially as a floor covering. **Goose** was the name given to a female who tended the geese. One example was Alice Gous, residing in Cornwall in 1297. **Gooseman** was the male counterpart of the name; one example was Gilbert Gosman who kept his watchful eye on the geese in Lancashire in 1246. Old English *calf* and *hierde* were put together to mean the man who looked after the calves. Warin le Calfhirde carried out this task in the county of Yorkshire in 1269. This has resulted in the surnames **Calvert** and **Calvard**.

The surnames **Grace**, **Gras** or **Grass** have several meanings. Those who acquired the surname through their occupation, like William atte Gras, were the people who put the cattle out to graze. Some acquired the name from the French *grace*, meaning one with a pleasing quality. Others, however, acquired the name from Old French *gras*, meaning fat. William Grace, a citizen of Colchester in 1310, was a grazier.

One set of surnames – **Scrimgeour**, **Skrinshire** and **Shrimshaw** – gives no clue at all as to their origins. The French *escremisseor* was a fencing master. In medieval England fencing schools were frowned upon and the sport was considered unsuitable. However, it must have occured as we have a record of Alexander Skrymchur, resident in Northampton in 1327.

Seller speaks for itself. It stems from Old English *sellan*, meaning to give or hand over, the name no doubt for a dealer or trader. Sanson Sellarius, a trader who lived in York in 1125, was fined for the illegal sale of arms.

Men have trodden the boards long before the time of Shakespeare. Old Norman *lekari* meant a player or actor, regarded in those days as a rogue. Richard Leyk trod the boards in London in 1292. Today the name is more respectable; we know it as **Laker**.

There are not many surnames which begin with the letter Q. One of these is **Quaife** or **Quaif**. It stems from Old French *coif* for a close-fitting hat, very popular in medieval times with French peasants and later introduced into England. Brian le Coyfier, recorded in the Essex Ripe Rolls for 1228, was no doubt a maker of these caps.

Among agricultural occupations the French *gardinier* described a gardener or someone working on a smallholding or fruit farm. Thomas and Rose Gardiner were a husband and wife team who worked in Suffolk in 1330. We now have among the many versions of the surname **Gardner**, **Gardinor** and **Gairdner**. Old English *pyrige* denoted a grower or seller of pears. Gilbert Perman, a City of London resident in 1376, was probably a fruit merchant. Since then the name has changed little, spelt today as **Pearman**. The medieval word *pekke* was given to a man who made pecks, vessels used as peck measures. Another City of London merchant was John de Peck, plying his trade in 1275. The surname remains as **Peck**. Still on the subject of measures, we have the surname **Gage** or **Gauge**, given to a man who was a tester or measurer. A female holder of the name, Alice Gage, resided in Colchester in 1310.

Although the number of occupations in medieval Britain was somewhat limited every man had his own job and never strayed into another worker's domain. There was still a vast variety of tasks carried out by working folk and officials. A very old trade is that of the stone mason, taken from Old French *machun*. The most popular areas for work for these craftsmen were the cathedral towns, where the work of building the cathedrals went on for centuries. Among the early craftsmen were Richard Machin, residing in Somerset in 1284, and Roger le Mason, working in Oxford in 1200. There are many variations of the surname, including **Mason**, **Machin** and **Masson**.

Old English *hlaffdigemann* was the term for a lady's servant. One such retainer was Geoffrey le Levediman of Guisborough. Passed down the centuries, it is known today as **Ladyman**. The similar surname **Maidment** stems from 'servant of the maiden'; William Maideman worked in Surrey in 1332. William le Yongeman of Clerkenwell, London, 1302, was described as a young servant. Today we spell his name **Youngman**.

Two more sedate occupations led to today's **Nutter** and **Latimer**. The first did not refer to a medieval 'yob'; it originated from Old English *notere*, meaning a scribe, writer or secretary. One such learned person was Robert le Notere, who scribbled away in Warwick in 1221. Old French *latinier* described an interpreter or speaker of Latin. One early linguist was Richard le Latener who spread the word in Essex in 1332.

Agriculture was the main occupation in medieval Britain. Old English *bonde* described a husbandman, peasant or churl. Later, under the Normans, it meant an unfree tenant or serf. Norman Bond lived in Warwickshire in 1180; his surname remains unchanged as **Bond**, although some variations are spelt **Bound** or **Bundy**.

Husbonda was an Old English term for a householder or farmer. Robert le Hosebonde, a resident of Cornwall, was mentioned in county records in 1279. Today his descendants are known as **Husband** or **Hosbond**. The term could also mean the young son of a farmer who took over the farm on his father's premature death. One such example was Robert le Yengehusbonde of Ely. Today it is spelt **Younghusband**.

One of the oldest occupations is that of the shepherd. The word stems from Old English *sceap-weard*. William Sepherd tended the flocks in the fields of Oxfordshire in 1279. The name now has many variations, including **Shepherd**, **Sheppard** and **Shippard**. The ancestors of either **Foreman** or **Fourmen** were not supervisors; it was Old English for swineherd. Although not a usual surname for women, we do find a Christina Foreman resident in Yorkshire in 1296. Geoffrey le Thressher toiled in the Essex wheatlands in 1319 as a thresher, leading to the surnames **Thresher** and **Thrasher**. **Orchard** needs no explanation: it described a man employed in an orchard, such as Richard atte Orchard, living in apple country in Worcester in 1316.

Old English *gyrd* meant a virgate, an old measure of thirty acres. The name Thomas de la Yurda described a man who held a yardland (a few acres of cultivated land). Centuries later the surname is spelt **Yarde** or **Yard**. The surnames **Vavasour** and **Vavaseur**, now among the less common surnames, were very popular centuries ago. They originated from Old French *vavasour* meaning a feuded tenant ranking just below that of a baron. In exchange for land held from the tenant-in-chief he provided men and horses for military purposes, and labour for agricultural work. Gilbert Le Vaussur was recorded in the Norfolk Pipe Rolls for 1167.

The surname **Flower** had nothing to do with being a florist; it stemmed from Old English *floer* – an arrow maker. William Flur followed his trade in York, as detailed in the Pipe Rolls for 1203. *Amel* meant an enameller. One holder of the name was William le Maillier, a citizen of Warwick, who carried out work for the king in 1203. The trade is still carried on today, and the surname continues as **Mailer**, **Maylor** or **Meyer**.

Baecere was Old English for a baker. William le Bakere turned out his loaves in Norfolk in 1177. The trade and name continues with **Baker** or **Backer**. If, as was often the case, the baker was female, such as Hanne Bakestre of Chester in 1260, it led to the surnames **Baxter** or **Bagster**.

Old English *geat* described a gate. In medieval times, when labour was cheap and plentiful, it was not uncommon to employ a man to guard or tend a gate. One such man was Hereward de Yette, a citizen of Gloucester in 1198. Today his descendants are known as **Yates**,

Yeates, or **Yetts**.

Old French *mire* described a physician. Herewardus le Mire Medicus tended his patients in Berkshire in the early part of the thirteenth century. The name has changed slightly, now being spelt **Myers** or **Miers**. Still on the subject of health, Old French *norrice* meant nurse. This was probably a female surname in the early days. Joan Norys was wiping the brows of her patients in 1379. The name is now **Nurse**, **Nurrish** or **Nourse**. Another surname with medical origins stemmed from Old English *leche*, meaning to cure. Walter le Lecher probably tended his patients in Hampshire towards the end of the thirteenth century. Now spelt **Letcher**, it seems an unfortunate label for such a noble profession. **Leach** was derived from Old English *laece* and described a physician. The records fail to tell us how many patients John Lache of Colchester, 1200, had or what his fees were.

Every village had its smithy, the centre of industrial activity for centuries, where any work connected with metal was carried out. Apart from the obvious surname of **Smith**, the village workshop threw up another surname. The French *ferour* described a worker in iron, or one who worked at the smithy. Hugo Farrour carried on his trade in the city of York in 1379. The modern versions of the name include **Farrow, Faro** and **Farrier**. **Ironmonger** is self-explanatory. It stems from old English *iren-mangere*. John le Irmongere carried out his trade in Oxford in 1255.

Old English *laedere* did not denote the leader of the pack but the driver of a cart, wagon or other vehicle used to transport coal or agricultural produce. Robert Cornlader, a resident of Colchester, was in charge of a corn wagon. This has produced three surnames, **Leader**, **Ledder** and **Lader**.

Cheese was an important and popular food in medieval England. *Wringan* meant a 'ringer' or presser of cheese. There was little doubt about the occupation of Richard le Chesewryngere, a tradesman in the City of London in 1281. The modern surnames **Ringer** or **Rainger** give little clue to their origins.

In medieval building work, the lashings used to tie the scaffolding were tightened by driving in wedges called *warrocks*. The nickname was given to the man who either erected the scaffolding or manufactured the warrocks. There may still be men engaged in the building trade today named **Warrick** or **Warrack**. Another name from the building industry, we find Robert le Shinglere, after *schinglen*, to cover with shingles, which were used on roofs. **Shingles** and **Shingler** are the modern versions. Stephen de Nailere, 1231, was a maker of nails. Today you will find them in the telephone book as **Naylor** or **Nailer**.

The man employed at a wharf or quay attracted the nickname *Key*, which was originally Cornish. John del Cay, a London resident in 1207, probably worked on one of the riverside quays. Although not a common surname the name today is **Kay**.

Among those carrying out civic duties we find **Keep** or **Keeper**, one employed at a keep or castle, sometimes a jailer. Simon Kepere was employed at a Sussex castle in 1327. **Bayliss**, **Bailey** and **Bayly** originated from a bailiff, a minor official of justice, who worked under the administration of a sheriff or warrant officer. One such official was Thomas Bailie, recorded in the Suffolk Subsidy Rolls for 1327. The French *justise* described a court official. William Justyse was a Norfolk constable in 1253. Down the years the name has changed to **Justice**.

Tollere described a tax gatherer. One such unpopular figure was John le Tollere who was a York citizen in 1251. The surname has become **Toller** and **Towler**. The surname **Kingsman** originated from the 'king's man', one who gave service to the king only, and not to some baron or lord. Godwin Kingesman carried out his royal duties in Norfolk in 1166. The church was closely related to the state and its officials were carefully chosen. Old English *deacon* described a church official who helped the priest. Later it described a layman attending to the secular affairs of the church. We have two early records of the surname, Richard le Diakne of Suffolk, 1212, and John Dekne, mentioned in Sussex records in 1327. Now the surname is spelt **Deacon** or **Deakin**.

On a lighter note the surnames **Sanger** and **Songer** originate from the medieval *songere*, given to a church singer or chorister. The surnames **Taber** and **Tabor** originate from the French *tabur*, a drum. No doubt Adam Tabur, a citizen of Shrewsbury in 1204, kept his fellow citizens on their toes. Old English *fuzelere* described a hunter of wild birds or a fowler. Robert de Fugler lurked in the marshes of Norfolk in 1227 when he was out seeking game. The name remains almost the same as **Fowler** or **Fugler**. Following a similar occupation was Coland le Ffauconer who in 1264 rented 26 acres in Walthamstow near London for rearing and training hawks. The name came from the French *fauconnier*. Today it is written as **Faulkner** or **Falconer**.

Dyer stems from Old English *deagere*, for a dyer, whilst **Wader** or **Weider** have older roots. The French called it *wesdier* but the English knew it as *woad*, a blue dye obtained from the plant of that name and still popular in the Middle Ages. The name was given to a man who manufactured or sold the dye.

The surname **Train** comes from the French *traine*, describing trickery, and was given to a man who used traps to catch wild animals. **Tanner** was the name given to a tradesman engaged in the leather industry. **Kiddle** or **Kidell** described someone who maintained or

32

manipulated a barrier, consisting of a dam or weir with openings for nets to catch fish. The name originated from the Anglo-French *kidel*, a wicker basket often used to catch fish. Simon Kidel, a Kentish man, lived on the banks of the Medway river and no doubt followed this occupation.

Wince was the Old English word for a pulley or winch used to draw water from a well or spring. Thomas atte Wynche of Worcester, 1332, was probably in charge of such a vital item of machinery, an important job as fresh water was a valued commodity in those days. Today those named **Winch** or **Winks** probably turn on a tap without a thought for their ancestors who carefully guarded the water supplies.

One surname associated mainly with women is **Threadgold** or **Tredgold**. There are at least seven variations of the surname, all stemming from the trade of embroiderer. Agnes Tredegold carried out her craft in Surrey in 1166.

In medieval times only the very wealthy owned a horse or could afford to hire mounted messengers, so many messages were carried on foot. Old French *trotier* described such a messenger. Robert Trotar resided in Hampshire in 1148 and was employed as the local messenger. Today the name is known as **Trotter**, **Trotman** or **Trott**.

Probably one of the most unusual occupations was that of the man who checked a measure of corn known as a quarter, which was about 28 pounds (12.7 kg). After the container or tub had been filled the man would level it off with a wooden stick called a *striker*. Reginald Le Strikere was probably employed by a London corn merchant in 1297. So if you have the surname **Strike** or **Striker** your ancestors are more likely to have worked in this trade than to have had anything to do with industrial action.

The fast food trade is not a recent development; it started centuries ago. Old French *potagier* described a maker or seller of pottage, a thick soup or broth. Walter de Potagier worked in the City of London in 1300. Today his descendants bear the name **Pottinger**.

Local surnames

Local surnames form by far the largest group. They derive from place names, indicating where a man lived or held land, or where he had been born. Some surnames originate from villages or hamlets that disappeared from our maps centuries ago, victims of the drift from agriculture to industry and the desire to live in bigger communities. In this chapter we shall look at surnames connected with place names in England.

A large number of local surnames come from tiny places such as single houses or manors, and often denote residence by a wood, in the marsh, or by oak, elm or ash trees. In the larger communities, men took their names from nearby inn signs, such as the sign of the Bell, or the Raven or the Ploughman.

A small hamlet in Lancashire called Renacres, or residence near the rye acres or the rye fields, was responsible for the surnames **Runacres**, **Runnacles** or **Runnicles**. Many of the early holders of the surname did come from Lancashire; others were from the eastern counties, famed for their rye. Alan de Ruynacres was mentioned in the Lancashire Assize Rolls for 1264, and Alice Renakers lived in Suffolk in 1568. The origin of **Uppington** is simple: Adam de Uppington lived in Uppington, Shropshire, in 1275. **Waterhouse** was derived from the dweller who lived in the house close to the water, or the inhabitant of a moated house. Adam del Waterhous was mentioned in the local records of Wakefield in 1308. There must be dozens of place names in England with the prefix Sand or Sandy. These places must be connected with the surnames **Sandell** and **Sandhill**, given to men who dwelt by the sandy slope or sandy hill. Thomas Attensands who lived in Yorkshire in 1301 possibly came from Sandhill, Yorkshire.

If your name is **Barclay** or **Berkeley** your family could have come from Berkeley in Gloucestershire, Berkley in Somerset, or Barklye in Sussex. The name was mentioned in the Domesday Book with a Roger de Berchelai who resided in Somerset. Richard de Flet who lived in Lincolnshire took his name from his native Fleet. Other families with the surname **Fleet** may have come from the same place or were dwellers by an estuary or a stream. **Ackland** was first formed from Old English *ac-land*, meaning the dwellers by the oak grove. William de Acklane who lived in Devon in 1275 probably had a beautiful view of a cluster of magnificent oak trees. Old English *pedant* described an enclosure, giving us the modern surname **Pallant**. One part of the ancient city of Chichester was known as the Pallant; it was here that John ate Palente lived in 1285. John Balam, one of the first of the **Balaam** family, acquired his surname through residence at Baylham,

Suffolk, in 1568. Our ancestors knew a pit or pool as a *seap* which eventually led to **Seath**. William Ateseth, mentioned in the Worcestershire Subsidy Rolls in 1275, probably lived by some deep pit or pool. **Tapp** originated from residence in Taplow, Buckinghamhire; the first holder of the name was Roger Tapp in 1247. The name has remained unchanged to this day. **Pitman** was the name given to a man who lived near a hollow, from the Old English *pyttmann.* The 1317 Assize Rolls for Kent mention a Walter Petman who lived near a hollow.

Residence near the town wall or the Roman wall naturally led to the surname **Wall**. Alexander le Wal lived near the town wall in Huntingdon in 1279. Hugo **Layfield** was a freeman of York in 1442. His ancestors had been given the surname as they must have lived near the 'lea field', the word for grasslands or pastures, and the name remains unchanged in its modern version. **Hampshire** needs no explanation. Thomas Hamshere of Kent, 1523, was given the name because he came originally from Hampshire. It was also given to a man who lived in Hallamshire, Yorkshire. John Hamshaw, a freeman of York in 1506, was born in this hamlet. Ely in Cambridgeshire was responsible for three surnames, **Ely**, **Heley** and **Eley**. Huna de Ely lived there in 1086 according to the Domesday Book. The name has remained unchanged for over nine hundred years. If your surname is **Ash**, **Dash** or **Tash**, or even **Naish** or **Nash**, then your ancestors all acquired their surname from Old English *aesc*, for a dweller by the ash tree or an inhabitant of one of the many places named Ash or Nash. There are more than eighty place names in England with the prefix Ash. Most of the early records of the surname come from places which were heavily wooded at the time; Hampshire and Sussex were two such counties. Ralph de Asche was mentioned in the Sussex Subsidy Rolls in 1296 and William Tasche was made freeman of York in 1599.

Richard de Inneshal who lived in Worcestershire in 1327 came from Insoll. The hamlet has long since vanished but lives on in the surname **Insole**. Another village which has vanished was Barraclough in Yorkshire; Peter del Baricloughe, mentioned in Wakefield records in 1316, came from here. Hundreds of Yorkshire families were endowed with the surnames **Barraclough** or **Barrowcliff**, a living link with a long-lost place.

Both **Venner** and **Fenner** were names for marsh dwellers. Among the first we find Walter le Veneur, recorded in the Devonshire Pipe Rolls for 1195. Adam de Wetecroft of Yorkshire, 1191, was the dweller by the croft where wheat was grown, today known as **Wheatcroft**. Richard Whetland of Sussex, 1327, lived by the wheatfield or wheatland; today his descendants are listed as **Wheatland** or **Wheatley**. The surnames **Alcott** and **Allcoat** are not so easy to guess. Thomas de Aldecote was mentioned in the Worcestershire Subsidy

Rolls for 1275. *Cote* was Old English for cottage and the name describes the man who dwelt at the old cottage. **Farncombe** and **Vearncombe** were both probably started by Robert de Ferncumb who resided in Farncombe, Surrey, in 1296. **Ingate** comes from Ingate in Suffolk. There was a Matilda de Endgate who lived there in 1327, while **Putnam** stemmed from residence in the villages of Puttenham in Hertfordshire and Surrey. A gentleman by the name of Ralph de Puteham lived in Berkshire in 1205 but records fail to reveal which Puttenham was his birthplace.

Grange was the Old French word for a granary or barn. William de la Graunge of Essex lived near a grange, which accounts for his name. We know it today as **Grange** or **Grainge**. Old English *ried* meant a clearing, and Roger de la Rede of Devon, 1208, lived in such a place. Another man with the same surname, Ralph de Rede, lived in Hertfordshire in the village of Reed in 1203. Other similar place names were Read in Lancashire and Rede in Suffolk. From these two origins sprang the surnames **Read, Reed**, **Redd** and **Reid**. The first Anglo-Saxon settlements were clearings in the forest, usually protected by a strong stockade, and this probably accounts for the frequency of the surname in its different forms. Another possible explanation is that reeds were used as floor coverings; it may have been given to the man who dwelt near the reeds.

Thomas atte Overe, mentioned in the 1275 Subsidy Roll of Worcester, acquired his name through residence near a steep bank or slope. Others named **Over** may have lived at Over in Cambridgeshire, Cheshire or Gloucestershire. Walter de Radecliua of Devon, 1182, was given the name because he lived near the red cliffs. His birthplace was known as Ratclyffe. Other places so named because of local red cliffs were Radclive in Buckinghamshire, Radcliffe in Lancashire and Nottinghamshire and Ratcliffe in Leicestershire and Nottinghamshire. It was from these places that the surnames **Radcliffe**, **Rackcliffe** and **Ratcliff** originated. Walter de Trobrigge, mentioned in the Gloucester Pipe Rolls for 1184, was born in Trowbridge, Wiltshire. Today, the surname is usually spelt **Trowbridge**, although another spelling is **Trubridge.** The surnames **Place** and **Plaice** were given to men who dwelt in the market place or similar enclosure. One of the earliest was John atte Place, mentioned in the Suffolk Feet of Fines (a list of taxpayers) in 1313.

George **Upsher** had his name included in the Suffolk Hearth Tax return for 1674; his name was taken from his birthplace of Upshire in Essex. Godwinus de Westuna, mentioned in the Domesday Book, acquired his name from one of the many Westons dotted about the country, giving us the surname **Weston**. But Alan Westerne, who resided in Suffolk in 1327, originally came from the West Country.

The modern spellings of his name are **Western** and **Wetron**. There are at least thirty-three places named Weston in England alone.

John Attele who lived in Berkshire in 1276 was given his surname because he lived in (*atte*) the *leah*, Old English for a clearing in the wood. The name was passed down, becoming **Atlay** or **Atlee** today, almost unchanged. **Fann**, **Vann**, or **Vance** all stem from Old English *fenn*, meaning marsh or fen, a common term in those days in Essex, Hertfordshire and Surrey. Richard de Fanne who lived in 1297 was a marsh dweller, probably living a very damp existence. **Dell** speaks for itself; Robert atte Delle of Sussex, 1296, was the dweller in the dell. Walter de Estgat, mentioned in the Norfolk Pipe Rolls of 1200, lived near the east gate of Norwich, hence the surname **Eastgate**. A different surname with a similar meaning is **Barr**. Medieval English *barre* meant barrier or gateway. John atte Barre lived by the town gate in Battle, Sussex, in 1288. The surname **Barrier** was given to a resident of Great Barr, Staffordshire. Another simple name is **Kendall**, derived from residence at Kendal in Cumbria. One of the first men with this name was John de Kendale in 1332. Richard de Meluer, mentioned in the Lancashire Assize Rolls for 1246, resided in Mellor, Lancashire, and the surname is still spelt **Mellor**.

People living on low-lying land or adjacent to a stream were referred to as folk living 'at ther ye'. In time this changed to 'at the rye', and rye was the name given to marshy places, the best known being Rye, Sussex. This in turn led to many surnames given to people living in marshy, isolated areas such as the Essex coast, Lincolnshire and parts of Sussex and Kent – **Rayman**, **Rea**, **Reaman**, **Ryman** and **Rye.** Robert Ryman, mentioned in the Sussex Subsidy Rolls for 1327, was a native of Rye, Sussex, a flourishing seaport at that time. John Rayman who dwelt in Essex in 1377 must have been a man of property to get his name on the county Assize Roll. William Stubbing of Norfolk, 1191, was the man who dwelt by the cleared land: the name has not changed much over the years. Today we write it as **Stubbings** or **Stubbins**. The town of King's Lynn in Norfolk has given us three surnames, **Lynn**, **Linn** and **Lenn**. One of the early inhabitants was Aedricus de Lenna who lived in the town in 1177. Robert de Felde, a native of Gloucester in 1185, was a Knight Templar who fought in the Holy Wars. His family resided near a cultivated field. Another family given the surname for the same reason was that of James atte Feld of Sussex, 1296. The modern equivalents are the surnames **Field**, **Delafield**, **Fields** and **Fielden**.

It would be difficult to find a surname more obviously connected with an area than **English** and **England**. There are three main areas for these surnames: the border country between England and Wales, and between England and Scotland; Lincolnshire and South Yorkshire;

and Essex, Kent and Sussex. In Wales and Scotland the name was given to a native from England, in Lincolnshire and South Yorkshire to a man who refused to adopt Danish customs, and in Essex, Kent and Sussex to the local population by the conquering Normans. It was used in the first place as a derogatory term, but later with respect. One of the many early holders of the name was John English of Kent who lived in 1317.

The counties of Kent, Somerset and Worcestershire are famed for their fruit-growing and the surnames of **Perry**, **Pirie** and **Perrie** have close connections with this ancient branch of horticulture. The surnames stemmed from Old English *pirige*, meaning pear, the nickname given to a man who lived near a pear tree or orchard. Henry le Peri lived in Somerset in 1176 while Richard Pirie resided in Kent in 1198. **Armistead** and **Armstead** come from a combination of the French *ermite* and Old English *stede,* giving us hermitage. Lawrence del Armetsted, mentioned in the Yorkshire Poll Tax returns for 1379, was described as the man who dwelt by the hermitage, the dwelling place of the hermit. At one time there were two small hamlets in Yorkshire called Barff and Barugh. These stemmed from the medieval English *bergh*, meaning hill, which is also the origin of surnames **Bargh**, **Barff** and **Barugh**, meaning the dweller by the hill. The first record of the surname comes perhaps surprisingly from Suffolk, one of our less hilly counties, with a Robert de Bargh, mentioned in the Feet of Fines for 1310.

The surname **London** presents little problem, and with it must be associated the names **Lundon** and **Lunnon**. These are among some very early surnames, usually given to men from London who settled in the country. Even in Anglo-Saxon times London was a city of great importance, and a Londoner settling elsewhere must have been treated with some respect. Aelfstan on Lundene lived in Kent in AD 988 and Leofsi de Lundonia was mentioned in the Domesday Book.

If your surname is **Norman** it does not mean that your ancestors were of Norman origin. The name was usually given to one who dwelt in the north, especially if he had been born in Norway.

Edmund de Ffeyrefeld lived in Kent in 1331. He was known as the man who dwelt by the fair land. Another origin for **Fairfield** was residence in one of the numerous places called Fairfield. The lost hamlet of Barnaby, Yorkshire, resulted in the surname **Barnaby**; one of the first holders was Richard de Bernaldeby who lived in Yorkshire in 1160. Richard Atte-Hill was so named in Shropshire in 1255 because he lived by a hill, hence the names **Athill** and **Athell**. The surnames **Shaw**, **Shave** and **Shea** derive from two sources, either the dweller by the wood, or men from Shaw in Wiltshire, Berkshire or Lancashire. John ate Shaw of Essex, 1295, was 'John who lived by the wood'. Both **Anstee** and **Anstey** were derived from residence at Anstey, and there are, or were, places with this name in Devon, Dorset, Hampshire, Hertfordshire and Wiltshire. Richard de Anesti, recorded in the Essex Pipe Rolls for 1164, probably owned land in one of these places and took the name when he moved to Essex.

We all know what a park is; the word comes from Old French *parc*, meaning enclosure. This gave us three surnames: **Park** was probably given to an Anglo-Saxon who lived near the park, while **Duparc** and **Dupare** were probably French names given to men who resided in the park as wardens or who owned the land. Henry del Parc, mentioned in the Somerset Assize Rolls for 1272, was probably a landowner and lived in his own park. He must have been a man of some means to be included in the Assize Rolls.

Both **Rand** and **Rance** originated from a place name, either Rand in Lincolnshire or North Yorkshire, or Raunds in Northamptonshire. One of the first records of the name, however, appeared in Suffolk in 1327 with Thomas Rande – no doubt a newcomer to the district who was born in one of the aforementioned places. Reginald de Seinesberia, recorded in the Gloucestershire Pipe Rolls for 1190, was born in Saintbury, Gloucestershire, hence his name, which we know today as **Sainsbury**. With a name like **Balderston** one could well imagine a bald ancestor, but the name, closely linked with **Boulderstone**, was derived from residence at Balderston in Lancashire. The first record of the surname is from Lancashire with William de Baldreston who resided in the county in 1292.

Many English place names bear the prefix Ham – the flat, low-lying land by a stream that made the ideal place for a settlement in Anglo-Saxon times. This prefix was also used as a surname to denote a man who lived near such an area, giving us **Ham** and **Hamme**. At first the surname was found chiefly in the south of England, especially in Sussex where Robert de la Hamme lived in 1275. A name very similar in spelling but with a different meaning is **Hulme**. Geoffrey de Hulm lived in Lancashire in 1202. The name was derived from residence at Hulme in Staffordshire, Cheshire or Lancashire.

With at least thirty examples, one of the most common English place names is Norton, which led to the surname **Norton.** Among the early holders of the name we find Walter de Northeton who lived in Norton near Chichester in Sussex in 1296. Thomas de Cliderhou resided in Clitheroe, Lancashire; by 1176 the family had moved to Yorkshire. Today, there is little doubt where the surname **Clitheroe** originated.

In the heart of Suffolk nestles the hamlet of Kersey, once famous for its watercress. One of its early residents was Adam de Kersey who moved a few miles away to Essex in 1325. The surname has remained unchanged, still spelt **Kersey**. **Bristow** began as the man from Bristol, which until the sixteenth century was known as Bristow – the site of the bridge. One early resident was Lia de Bristov, mentioned in city records in 1191. William ater Bregg, a Sussex resident in 1296, was described as the man who dwelt near the bridge. Little has changed: the surname today is **Bridges**. Old Norman *kjarr* meant wet ground. It was given to the man who dwelt near the marsh or land noted for flooding. One example, William Carre, a citizen of Oxford in 1279, may have dwelt near meadows close to the river. One hopes that those named **Carr** today do not suffer from these residential hazards. Another common English place name is Coat or Cote, found in Somerset, Oxfordshire, Lincolnshire and Leicestershire. It was taken from Old English *cot*, meaning cottage or shelter. The nickname was given to the man who was living in the cottage or the man living near the sheep cote. There are several versions of the surname, including **Coats**, **Cottis** and **Cotes**.

There are two origins for the surname **Abraham**. One is from the Hebrew for high father, a name not confined to the Jewish race. The other stems from residence at Abram, Lancashire. John de Abburgham was mentioned in the Lancashire Assize Roll for 1246. There is no doubt about the surnames **Shrewsbury** or **Shrosbree**; they originate from the Shropshire town of Shrewsbury. One of its early citizens was John Shrouesbury in 1280. Two tiny hamlets, Ifold in Sussex and Ifield in Kent, gave us the surnames **Ifold** and **Ifield**. Benedict de Ifold lived in the Sussex village at the end of the thirteenth century.

Waltham Holy Cross in Essex, site of the abbey which was founded by King Harold before the Norman Conquest, is reputed to be the burial site of the last Anglo-Saxon king. John de Waltham, no doubt born in the village, moved to nearby Colchester in 1119. The surname remains unchanged, still spelt **Waltham**.

An unusual surname is **Plank**, derived from Old English *planke*, the dweller by the plank or narrow bridge. A well-founded Yorkshire surname was obtained from the place name Jervaulx. At one time it was Gervaus before changing to its present spelling. Very common in York, family members were freemen of York for centuries, from John Gerveux, 1360, to Thomas Jarvis, 1713. There are at least six versions of the surname, including **Jarvis** and **Gervaise**.

Michael de Sevenoke lived in the Kentish market town in 1258. Now both town and surname are spelt **Sevenoaks**. Richard de Routhesthorn found his name in the Lancashire Assize Rolls for 1246; he was a resident of Rostherne, Cheshire. Many citizens must have left this place taking the town as their surname as there are at least twelve ways to spell the surname. Three of them we know today as **Rawsthorn**, **Rosten** and **Rosthorn**.

There are two Quintons, one in Gloucestershire, the other in Worcestershire, meaning 'queen's manor'. The surname has remained unchanged for more than eight hundred years, still spelt **Quinton**. There can be few doubts about the origins of **Pontefract**, which means 'place near the broken bridge'. Willelmus de Pontefracto lived in the Yorkshire town in 1197 when it was still known as Pontefracto.

Durandus de Gloucestre was mentioned in the Domesday Book as a land holder in Gloucester. The surname has changed only slightly, known today as **Gloster**. Ralph del Bec, an Essex resident in the thirteenth century, was so called because he lived near the brook. It has changed little, written in this day and age as **Beck**. The prefix Bery or Bury is common in English place names: Berry Pomeroy in Devon (the second part of the name added by the Pomeroy family who were given the manor after the Battle of Hastings), Bury St Edmunds in Suffolk, and a Bury in Hampshire and in Lancashire. The name stems from Old English *byrig* or *beri* meaning enclosure dweller. Residence in an enclosure of fort led to the surnames **Berry**, **Bury** or **Burgh**.

The place name Worth in Kent and Sussex gave rise to the surname **Worth**. In Anglo-Saxon times the village or hamlet was an enclosed farm. John de Wurde had moved a short distance from the village by 1195, but William de Werthe was still living in the Sussex village in 1275.

Aldridge was once a tiny hamlet in Staffordshire but is now a suburb of Walsall. Drogo de Alrewic lived in the locality in 1201. Although the place itself has changed dramatically the surname has changed little and is today written as **Aldrich**.

The surname **Bell** was given to the man who lived near the sign of the bell outside an inn of that name or to one who dwelt by the church or town bell, or near a bellhouse. Probably John atte Bell, a City of London resident in 1332, had only to pop next door for a drink.

First recorded in AD 678, Inkpen is a small village nestling in the shadow of the Berkshire Downs, with nearby Inkpen Beacon the highest point on the Downs. This Anglo-Saxon settlement has given us the surnames **Inkpen** and **Ingpen**.

Bowden, or 'Bucge's settlement', comes from an Anglo-Saxon woman who also gave her name to Bowden, Devon. John le Boghedon resided near the village in 1333. A few miles from Harrogate, North Yorkshire, perched out on the moors, is the tiny hamlet of Bland Hill. There is little doubt why the Anglo-Saxons named this place *gebland*, the windy place. Few people chose to live in such an exposed place, but a surprising number of inhabitants ended up with the surname **Bland**.

Dalton is a common place name especially in the north, in Durham, Lancashire, Northumberland, Cumbria and Yorkshire. If your surname is **Dalton** or **Daughton** your ancestors could have sprung from any of these places. William le Daltone dwelt in Durham in 1155.

There are dozens of place names with the prefix Combe. Apart from residence in one of those places, the surnames **Comber** or **Coomer** may have originated from 'dweller in the valley'. William le Combere was a villager in the hamlet of Coombe on the north Devon coast in 1260.

The town of Hastings was named after Haesta, an Anglo-Saxon chief. It has given its name to one of the decisive battles in British history. By coincidence, the Old English name *Haesta* means violent or fight. Evidently the tribe which settled in this area was renowned for its violence. Robert de Hastinges lived in the town in 1086. Although not common, the surname **Hastings** is still found.

The surname **Appleton** is derived from a place of that name in Cheshire, Berkshire, Yorkshire or Kent. It may also have been given to someone who resided near an apple orchard. This probably applied to Thomas ate Napeltone who in 1317 resided in Kent, known as the 'garden of England' and famed for its apple orchards. **Maples** denoted the man who dwelt by the maple trees. John Mapel lived in the county of Cornwall in 1327.

Originating in north-east England, the surname **Nesbit** was acquired through residence at Nesbit in Northumberland or Nesbitt in Durham. One Durham resident was William de Nesebite who lived in the city in 1250.

Norwich has two origins: a resident of the city of that name or the dweller at the dairy farm situated north of the village or hamlet. Goscelinus de Norwic was firmly settled in the city by 1086, rewarded with lands in the area for services rendered at the Battle of Hastings.

Thomas de **Grantham** resided in the town of that name in 1220. The place name originated as 'Granta's ham' and also resulted in the surname **Grant**. From the town on the river Medway in Kent we get the surname **Rochester**. One of the earliest holders of the name, Turoldus Rouecestra, must have crossed the Thames from Kent into Essex by 1086 when he was recorded as an Essex land holder.

A very common place name, Stratford meant a place where a Roman road crossed a river. Robert de **Stratford** resided in Stratford St Mary, just north of Colchester, in 1086. The surname still remains unchanged after more than nine centuries. There is no confusion over the origins of **Devon**. It described a man who hailed from that county. Adam de Devoun had left his birthplace and settled far away in Norfolk by 1275. Old English *fiscgear* described an enclosure for catching fish, and someone who lived close to the site, probably near a river, soon attracted the surname that we know today as **Fisher**.

Old English *spryng* meant a spring or well. The Normans had the word *fontaine* for the same thing. A man who lived near such a site soon attracted the surname. John de Funtayne who lived in Essex in 1270 was fined for some unrecorded misdemeanour. We now know his descendants as **Fountain** or **Fontaine**.

The surnames **Idle** and **Idell** do not necessarily indicate an ancestor with lazy habits. Some members of the family lived in Idle in Yorkshire or Idle in Nottinghamshire. John Del Idle, a citizen of York in 1301, found himself on the Assize Roll for that year.

Some folk may have acquired the surname **Crook** or **Krook** from the uncomplimentary Danish nickname *krok*, referring either to a sly or cunning person, or to one with a crooked back. However, the surname was also acquired through residence at Crook, Durham, or at other places with the prefix Crook in the name.

There is a **Crowhurst** in Sussex and another in Surrey. The Sussex village was established long before the Norman invasion and supplied the majority of the surnames. William de Crouherst resided in the area in 1296.

Both Wheatacre, a hamlet near Beccles in Suffolk, and the twin villages of Nether and Over Whitacre near Birmingham gave birth to the surnames **Whitaker** and **Widdaker**. We have early records of the surname from each region. Simon de Witacr resided in Warwickshire in 1180 and John de Wheteacre was recorded in the Suffolk Subsidy Rolls for 1327.

There is no doubt about the origins of the surname **Worcester**; the first holders of the surname came from that city. Later, the surname became **Wooster** and **Wostear**. One citizen was William de Worcester, mentioned in the county Assize Rolls for 1290.

The two hamlets of Headbourne Worthy and Kings Worthy are near Winchester in Hampshire. These villages are amongst the oldest Anglo-Saxon settlements still in existence. They have produced one of the oldest surnames in the English language, **Worthy**. Godwine at Wordige was mentioned in Anglo-Saxon records in the year AD 826. Also in Hampshire, on the edge of the New Forest is the village of Ower, which has given the surname **Owers**. Much further north, there is a Whaley in Derbyshire and a Whalley in Lancashire which generated the surnames **Whalley** and **Whaley**. Searching back we find Adam de Walleg from Lancashire in 1185 and Richard de Wailey of Derby in 1230.

In one of the wildest and most remote parts of Cumbria are Muncaster Fell and Castle. Centuries ago there was a small hamlet here where once a Roman fort had stood. The place still lives on with descendants of its former inhabitants scattered across the country with the surnames **Mulcaster** and **Muncaster**.

The dweller by the rowan tree soon attracted the surname of

Rowntree or **Roundtree**. Robert Rountre, a citizen of York, found his name in the Assize Roll for 1301. One wonders if he was an ancestor of the family later to become famous for their chocolate. Still in the north of England, Sowerby is a common place name originating from the Norman *saurr*, meaning mud or dirt; it referred to a farm or village near marshy land. Cumbria, Lancashire and Yorkshire have all had villages or hamlets with this name. Residents in these localities passed on the surnames **Sowerby**, **Sorbie** and **Sorby**. Odierna de Sourebi lived in Cumbria in 1195.

Among the lesser known surnames we find **Umpleby** and **Umplebye**, which arose in the hamlet of Anlaby on the outskirts of Hull. A few years later the surname had found its way to Leeds and Bradford. William de Anlauby was a York citizen in 1289.

As for **Radbourne** or **Radbone**, there are a number of places where the surname first originated: Radbourn in Warwickshire, Radbourne in Derbyshire, Redbourn in Hertfordshire and Redbourne in Lincolnshire. The place names all mean 'where the reeds grow'. One single surname, **Upton**, originated from one of at least thirty localities with that name. It stemmed from Old English *upp-tun*, meaning the higher farm or homestead. One of the first to bear the name was Ethestan on Optune, resident in Northamptonshire nearly a century before the Norman Conquest.

Old English *birce*, meaning birch, was given to the man who dwelt by the birch trees. Walter de la Birche resided in Worcester in 1182. The name has changed little since, today written as **Birch**.

The surname **Law** had no links with the legal profession. It sometimes originated from Old English *hlaw* for a hill or burial mound. It became **Low** in the south, but remained **Law** in the north. Medieval English had the word *clough* which meant a 'dweller in the fair hollow'. The surnames **Fairclough**, **Faircliff** and **Faircloth** stemmed from this description and are common throughout England. Simon de Ffairclogh was mentioned in the Lancashire Subsidy Rolls for 1332, whilst Robert Fayreclought resided in Saxmundham in 1368.

There are least ten spellings of the surname **Goldstone** or **Gulson**. They all first appeared in two lost hamlets, Goldstone in Kent and another in Shropshire. Ambrose Golson was a member of the Kentish branch of the family, living in the county in 1523. Wetheral in Cumbria acquired its name as the place where *wethers* (farm animals) were kept. This village, on the outskirts of Carlisle, created the surnames **Wetherall**, **Witherell** and **Wetherill**. By 1332 Richard de Wederhal had moved from the village to the comparative comfort of Carlisle.

A long lost place name, Underhill, resulted in the surname **Underhill** or **Undrell** for one who lived at the foot of the hill. Robert de Underhull found his name in the Somerset Assize Roll for 1268. The surname **Kentish** is self-explanatory. It was the name given to someone who came from the county that was first known as *Cantium* by the Romans, then *Cantia* by the Anglo-Saxons, then *Centiac*. Later variations of the surname were **Cantes** and **Kintish**. By 1332 the family of Richard Kentissh had moved over the border into Sussex.

Although the surname **Hatch** mainly originated from villages of that name in Bedfordshire, Hampshire, Somerset and Wiltshire, a few families acquired the name through residence near a hatch or gate, usually leading to a forest or woodland. Perhaps Adam de Hach, resident in Norfolk in 1212, had the task of guarding the gate leading to the forest.

The unusual surname **Rome** or **Room** was given to a man who was either an immigrant from the 'eternal city' or perhaps a pilgrim who had visited Rome. If John de Rome, a citizen of York in 1379, had visited Rome it would have been quite an achievement.

John atte Hirne, living in Sussex in 1327, may have acquired his name through residence near a nook or a corner of land, or even near a bend in a river, road or lane. Herne in Kent was named after its location in a curving valley. There is also a Hurn in Hampshire. The surname today is **Hearne** or **Hurne**. From Lach Dennis, a tiny village in Cheshire, or from residence near a stream, the surname **Latch** evolved. Christiana de Lech resided in Northleach in Gloucestershire in 1210. Other variations of the surname include **Leche** and **Leech**.

The place names Roade in Northamptonshire, Rhode in Devon and Road in Somerset all mean 'the settlement in the clearing in the woods'. This led to the surname **Rhodes** or **Roads**, usually denoting that the holder came from one of these places. Old English *haga*, the dweller by the enclosure, and the place name Haigh in either Lancashire or Yorkshire have resulted in the surname of **Haigh** or **Hague**.

Old Norman *skali* meant a hut or temporary dwelling. It became both a place name and a surname. Scales in Cumbria and in Lancashire, Scole in Norfolk and Scholes in Yorkshire were all responsible for the surnames **Scales** and **Scholes**. Two early examples are Thomas de Scales, residing in Cumbria in 1332, and John de Scholes, a resident of Leeds in 1379.

The tiny Devon hamlet of Northcott on the road to Holsworthy was responsible for the surnames **Northcott** and **Norkutt**. One local resident was Nicholas de Northicote who resided in the area in 1199. **Witham** originated either from Witham in Essex or from an isolated hamlet near Bourne in Lincolnshire called Witham on the Hill. Probably the majority of families came from the Essex town, such as those of Peter de Wytham, 1295, and John Witham, 1327.

Wardle, the name of a hamlet in Cheshire and of a suburb of Walsall, is responsible for the surnames **Wardle**, **Wardale** and

Wardell. By 1218 Thomas de Wardhill had moved to Lancashire and was affluent enough to be included in the county Assize Rolls.

Old English *haeo* described the 'dweller on the heath', and as much of medieval England was uncultivated heathland the surname could have originated from almost any part of the country. A few place names have the prefix Heath. Laurence atte Hethe resided in Heathfield, Sussex, in 1296. The surname is now spelt **Heath**.

The surname **Tonbridge** has more than one origin. Some people acquired it through residence in the Kentish town, such as Richard de Tonebrigg, 1086. Others were so called through residence near a bridge by the village.

In medieval England few people could read and signs indicated many establishments, including inns. The surname **Raven** was probably given to a man who lived near the sign of the raven. William atte Raven was a City of London merchant in 1344.

There are at least nine ways of spelling the surname **Fawcett** or **Fossett**. It is a typical northern surname, numerous in Yorkshire, where it arose in the small hamlet of Forcett. Others came from Fawcett in Cumbria, or Facit in Lancashire. John del Ffanside was still living in his native Cumbria in 1332, and Richard Fascet had become a freeman of York by 1398.

The surname **Ford** or **Forth** denoted a man who either lived near a ford or river crossing, or resided in one of the many places named Ford. There are at least ten, including those in Somerset, Herefordshire and Sussex, from where there is a record of Geoffrey atte Forde who resided in the district in 1296. Another common place name provided the surname of **Ashford**. Reginald de Asford was an inhabitant of the village of Ashford Carbonel near Ludlow in 1221.

Calver was a hamlet in the Derbyshire Peak District and meant 'where the calves graze'. It provided the surname **Calver**. David de Calvenore was a villager in 1200. Quarrington in Lincolnshire gave rise to **Quarrington**, whilst the surname **Langhurst** or **Longhurst** came from Old English *hyrst* for a long wooded hill. Some families may have come from Longhirst, Northumberland.

Several localities provided the surnames **Lund** and **Lount**. Among them are Lund in Yorkshire, Lunt in Lancashire and Lound in Lincolnshire, Nottinghamshire and Suffolk. One member of the Yorkshire branch of the family was Ralp de la Lundie, recorded in the Yorkshire Pipe Rolls for 1183. The surname **Lomas** or **Lummis** began in Lomax, previously *Lumhalghs*, which used to be in Lancashire. The earliest record of the name is Richard Lomax, a citizen of Preston in 1602. Exhall near Coventry gave us the surnames **Exall**, **Excell** and **Exell**. Richard de Ecleshal dwelt there in 1221.

There are dozens of place names with the prefix Stoke, all denoting dependance on a nearby manor. From these communities sprang the surnames **Stokes**, **Stook** and **Stoakes**. Ricerus de Stochas resided in Stoke, a hamlet near Hartland Point in Devon, in 1084.

A surname that reaches back long before the Norman Conquest was taken from Bygrave, a small hamlet near Baldock in Hertfordshire. Leommaer aet Biggrafan was mentioned in the Anglo-Saxon Chronicles in 1015. Today we know the surname as **Bygraves**, **Bigrave** or **Bygreaves**.

Local surnames of French origin

The Domesday Book was commenced in 1086 at the instigation of William the Conqueror. He sent his clerks and officials into every part of England to begin the gigantic task of stocktaking on a national scale. The work was as competent and as accurate as any modern survey. Part of the wealth of information contained in the two volumes that make up the Domesday Book are accurate details of the landowners. The majority of the tenants-in-chief and the sub-tenants were Norman, French or Breton, rewarded for their services at the Battle of Hastings. Altogether, some two hundred barons and four thousand knights were thus recompensed.

The distribution of these lands was influenced by two factors. Firstly, the danger points (the Sussex, Kent and East Anglian coasts, the northern and Welsh borders, and other vulnerable areas) were given to trustworthy men, sometimes kinsmen of the king, who were as much military commanders as landowners, charged with the safety of the realm. Secondly William was concerned about internal law and order. He ensured that no baron was placed in a position where he could mount a successful rebellion backed by an entire countryside in his economic power. The barons therefore had their land spread out over England, a manor here, a manor there.

Many of these landowners and their followers took as a second name their birthplace, which eventually became their surname. If your surname is derived from a French place name, it does not mean, however, that your ancestors arrived with William the Conqueror as English workers employed on the estates later adopted their lord's surname. In addition, some years after the Conquest, large numbers of French immigrants arrived and many of these adopted the name of their home town as their surname. Very few of the original French landowning families survived; the land was split up and sold many times during the next few centuries. Two hundred years after the Conquest it was hard to distinguish those of Norman birth from those born in England. Contemporary writings reveal a new pride in England and its native traditions. The Anglo-Norman period had begun.

One of the Norman knights who settled in East Anglia was Hugo de Bellcamp from Beauchamps-la-Manche, mentioned in the Hertfordshire division of the Domesday Book. Today the surname lives on as **Beauchamp** and **Beecham**. Robert de Beauchamp who lived in Essex in 1203 claimed that his ancestors came from another Beauchamp in France. Similar in name are **Beaufoy** and **Buffey**, first mentioned in the Domesday Book as Ralph del Bellafago, resident in Norfolk and Suffolk. A later member of the family was Thomas Buffy of Oxford, 1276. These families owe their surname to their birthplace of Beaufour. Eustace de Lorreyne who resided in Scotland in 1333 originally came from Lorraine. The modern surname is **Lorrain**. Philip de Chailewai, mentioned in the Gloucester Pipe Rolls for 1165 came from Caillouet. He owned a manor in Wiltshire named Kellaways. The name is the forerunner of today's **Calloway** and **Kelway.**

The **Mountjoy** family was one that arrived after the Conquest, probably among the large number of French who arrived some forty or fifty years after the Norman invasion. Gilbert de Montgoye, mentioned in the Yorkshire Assize Rolls for 1219, was a man of property; he acquired his name from his birthplace – Montjoie. Another family whose name came from a place was that of Montigni La Manche; today the surname is known as **Mountney**. Very similar are **Mountford**, **Montford** and **Mumford**. Hugo de Montford, mentioned in the Domesday Book, was an under-tenant who had arrived with William. His birthplace was Montford-sur-Risle. Another branch of the family was represented by Simon de Mumford, mentioned in the Kentish Feet of Fines for 1242. Also rewarded for his services at Hastings was Ralph de Pomerai, recorded in the Domesday Book as a tenant-in-chief in Devon. He left his name in the village of Stockleigh Pomeroy. In 1225 the family was still there, headed by Henry le Pomereie. Their home town was La Pommeraye, meaning the town near the apple orchard. People named **Pomeroy** or **Pummery** may care to visit Stockleigh Pomeroy if they are in Devon.

Robert de Montealo, who lived in Scotland in 1214, and Richard de Mohaud of Yorkshire, 1208, are forerunners of those who today bear the surname **Mowatt**. Both men came from Montaut, which gave them their surname. William de Cadomo, recorded in the Domesday Book as holding lands in Suffolk, originated from Caen; his descendants are known as **Camm**. Another link with this Norman city was in Dorset, where the abbey of Caen owned large estates.

Among the church establishments which owned vast lands given by William was the abbey of Saint Pierre-de-Semilly. In the Feet of Fines for Northumberland published in 1256 we find Richard Saunper, whose ancestors were named after their birthplace at Saint Pierre. The name has changed slightly; today we spell it as **Semper** or **Samper**. They could almost be confused with **Santler** and **Sandler**, but these families originated from Saint Hillaire or Saint Lo. Among early records we find Robert de Sancto Elerio of Lancashire, 1219, and Geoffrey de Sancto Laudo who resided in Hampshire in 1148. Anketillus de Furnels of Cornwall and Odo de Fornelt of Somerset were both mentioned in the Domesday Book as under-tenants. Richard de Furneals who resided in Hertfordshire gave his name to Furneux, similar to the birthplace of his ancestors – Fourneaux. The surname has changed very little; today we spell it **Furneaux**. A name that has remained unchanged since it was first written in the Domesday Book is **Vaux**, closely connected with **Vause**. Robert de Vals de Vaux owned lands in Norfolk; his home town was Vaux, a common French place name. A later member of the family was Richard de Vause, resident in Leicester in 1200.

The surname **Moon** has nothing to do with ancient astrologers. William de Moin, a Domesday Book under-tenant with lands in Dorset, originally came from Moyon; the family was still going strong in Somerset in 1239 with Reginald de Moun. **Vallis** was first recorded in 1275 in Suffolk with Sibil de Valeyse. Her family came from Valois. The name **Venables** came from a French town called Vanables; our first record comes from Lancashire in 1200 with William de Venables. Robert de Glanvilla, under-tenant in Norfolk, came from Glanville in France. Today the surname is written exactly as the town was spelt – **Glanville**.

One could hardly think of a more unlikely candidate for a French surname than **Poggs**, but Imbert la Pugeys arrived in England in 1236, a court official who accompanied Eleanor, Henry III's queen. He came from Le Puy-en-Valay, and left his name in Stoke Poges, Buckinghamshire. **Baskerville**, made famous by Sir Arthur Conan Doyle, originated in Boscherville; our first record mentions Roger de Baschervilla, a resident of Gloucester. Neither **Havill** nor **Hovell** has anything to do with living in sub-standard accommodation. Ralph de Halvile, a Domesday tenant-in-chief, owned vast estates in Worcestershire; before sailing with William he lived at Hauville.

Goisfridus de Magna de Manneville was in the thick of the battle at Hastings, and displayed great personal courage. His reward was to become tenant-in-chief of vast lands in Essex and Kent, and from this branch of the family came the first Earls of Essex. From this beginning grew the surnames **Mandeville**, **Manville** and **Manwell**. The Essex Mandevilles came from Manneville, the Buckinghamshire and Devon branches came from Magneville, while others were from Manne-Ville-sur-Risle. One of the first of the Buckinghamshire family was William de Manevell who lived in the county in 1210. Another family made tenant-in-chief in return for services rendered at the Battle of Hastings was William de Perci. His estates were mostly in Yorkshire. He was under-tenant to Hugh, Earl of Chester, and his second line of succession took the surname **Percy**, while others became known as **Pursey**. The original family came from Percy-en-Auge. A branch of the family that settled in Sussex was that of Henry Percy, mentioned in county records in 1332.

Some of the scenes of action in the First and Second World Wars were the homes of men who have left surnames to us. One such place was Cambrai, from where Goderfridus de Cambrai left to fight for William. His reward was an estate in Leicestershire. Another member of the family was living in Sussex in 1296; his name was Simon **Cambray**. Hugo de Montgomeri was given lands in Somerset for his part in the battle. The name appeared again in 1159 with William de Mungumeri who resided in Stafford. **Montgomery** and **Montgomerie** descend from one of two French place names, Sainte-Foy-de-Montgomery or Sainte-German-de-Montgomery.

A Celtic place name has given us **Deveraux**, **Everist** and **Deverose**. Roger de Ebrois, who did very well out of the Norman invasion, settled in Norfolk with more than enough land for his needs. His birthplace was Evreux, from a Celtic name meaning the tribal dwellers on the Ebura river. Petrus de Valdinges settled in Cornwall after the invasion; the modern surname is **Vallin**, the original birthplace Valognes. Another branch of the family was represented in Kent by John de Valin who lived in the county in 1237. Rogerius de Belmont divided his time between Dorset and Gloucester. If your name is **Beaumont** or **Belmont**, your ancestors may have come from Beaumont-le-Roger, home of the original sub-tenant. The name was again mentioned in Suffolk in 1300 with John Bomund, a local land-owner.

Among the less common surnames we find **Sackville** and **Sackwild**, now mostly connected with the peerage. Richard de Sachevilla, mentioned in the Domesday Book as a landowner in Hertfordshire and Essex, originally came from Sauqueville-Seine, hence his surname. Another holder of the name was Alexander de Saccaville who resided in the City of London in 1162. Neither **Bethune** or **Beaton** can claim an entry in the Domesday Book; the first record of the family dates from 1195 with Baidwinus de Betton, living in Berkshire. This family came from Bethune near the Pas-de-Calais region. **Montague** is the surname of at least five titled families and, at the same time, a surname held by people of all walks of life. De Montagud, a Domesday Book tenant, held lands in Somerset; he came from Montaigu-le-Bois. Other holders of the name may have come from Montaigu-la-Manche. The surname has given itself to a village to the west of Yeovil in Somerset; Montacute is the Latin version, and Shepton Montague the French version.

During Anglo-Saxon times a Welsh bishop crossed to Brittany and founded the abbey of Dol. The name of Bishop Samson was reintro-duced into England by Bretons, who took the surnames of **Sampson**, **Samson** or **Sanson**. Other Frenchmen, born in one of three places called Saint-Samson, may also be responsible for introducing the surname.

If your surname is **Lisle**, **Lile** or **Lyle**, or any of these with the prefix De, there is a variety of birthplaces from where your ancestors may have come. Isle was a common French place name, and other men with one of these surnames may have come from Lille. Hunfridus de Insula of Worcester managed to get his name in the Domesday Book and Robert del Ile was a freeman of York in 1311.

Among the early Norman families who settled in and near London we find the name **Berners.** Hugo de Berneres arrived with William and held lands in London, Middlesex and Essex. He came from Bernières. The family was still living in London in 1185 with one Goda de Berners who fought in the Holy War. There were two places called Dampierre in Normandy, probably the birthplace of some of the French immigrants who arrived after the Conquest. It gave us the names **Dampier** and **Damper**. Among early records we find William de Damper who was leading a peaceful life in York around 1225. One could write a whole chapter on the subject of Mowbray and its associated surnames, **Moubray**, **Mulberry** and **Membry**, and **Memery**, **Mowbury** and **Memory**. All these various families have one birthplace in common – Montbrai-la-Manche. As the first holders of the name were wealthy landowners, the surname may have been adopted by men who worked on their estates. Rodbeard a Mundbraeg was mentioned in the Anglo-Saxon Chronicles in 1087. Paganus de Moubrai resided in Oxford in 1150 while Roger de Munbrai, a resident of Lincolnshire with lands in Yorkshire, was a Knight Templar and fought in the Holy War. But the family made its biggest mark in Leicestershire, giving its name to the town of Melton Mowbray, and a quick glance at the freemen of Leicester will show how powerful this clan was in the county. John Mowbray was a freeman of Leicester in 1714; others include John Memory, 1725, and John Membry, 1748. It is interesting to note they all had the same forename.

The name **Angwin** descends from 'the man from Anjou'; Godfrey Aungewin lived in Somerset in 1247. **Venes**, **Venis** and **Venus** come from Venoix; the first holder of the name was Robert de Venuiz in 1130 in Hampshire. **Bewes** came from Bayeux, home of the famous tapestry; William Baives, 1235, was a Berkshire landowner.

Ross is mentioned twice in the Domesday Book, firstly as simply Rozo, and secondly with Serlo de Ros, under-tenant in Kent and Bedfordshire. These men came from Rots in the province of Calvados. **Marris** and **Mares** have nothing to do with horses; the original families came from Le Marais, meaning the town by the marsh. The family is mentioned twice in the Domesday Book – Clarenbodo de Maresc, with lands in Berkshire, and Richard de Maris, an under-tenant in Kent. Thomas de Saint Vigor, mentioned in the Somerset

Assize Roll for 1268, was a descendant of a French immigrant family from Saint Vigor in the province of La Manche. The surnames have changed somewhat down the centuries; today we spell them **Savager** and **Savigar**.

Early members of the **Grenville** or **Grenfell** family were quiet, peaceful French merchants who settled in England some years after the Conquest. They left their native Grainville-la-Teinturière and settled in York. One of the family, William de Grenefell, became a freeman of York in 1363. **Damary** and **D'Amery** are part of a group of surnames that also includes **Amory** and **Amori**. The family is mentioned in the Domesday Book with William de Dalmari of Dorset who had come from Daumeray, in the province of Maine-et-Loire.

At first sight anyone with the surname **Spain** would assume that his or her ancestors had not come from France at all. The name refers to Epaignes in Normandy or Espinay in Ille-et-Vilaine, however. Aluredus De Hispania, recorded in the Domesday Book, came from Epaignes. Thomas Spane, resident in York in 1302, was a Breton onion seller.

The surname **Rivers** did not originate from dwelling near a river or stream. The first members of the family hailed from La Rivière near Calais. They are mentioned in the Domesday Book as De Rivaria, holding land in Somerset, so it may be assumed that they arrived with William the Conqueror.

One of the most battle-scarred places in the First World War was Picardy, the region around Amiens and the Somme. A man who left this area more than nine centuries ago soon acquired the surname **Pickard** after his arrival in England. The family was well established by the time Hugh Le Pycard had his name entered in Somerset records in 1276. Another place name which is a grim reminder of the First World War is Flanders. Thomas Flandres who resided in Somerset in 1327 owed his name to his ancestors' birthplace. Passed down the years, the surname has now become **Flanders** and **Flinders**.

Those Norman families who hailed from the Calais area did not have to travel far to reach their adopted home. The **Quincy** family came from Cuincht, Pas de Calais. Saer De Quincy who lived in Oxford in 1153 was the ancestor of the Earls of Winchester.

From Viller or Villier, both common French place names, we get the surname **Villiers**. Roger de Vilers, living in Dorset in 1166, came from Villers-la-Sec, Normandy. Another family that arrived with William the Conqueror was that of Hugo de Quintino who received lands in Hampshire as a reward for his services. The first **Quinton** family arrived from St Quentin near Cherbourg. Later holders of the surname may have arrived from St Quentin-en-Tourmont in the Somme area.

There are several communities named Campagne in Normandy. William Campaignes who lived in Dorset in 1200 came from one such place. The name is shorter now and is spelt **Campen**. From Soissons, north-east of Paris, came Rufus de Sessuns who settled in Berkshire. More French than Norman, the surname today is **Sessions**.

It is reasonably safe to assume that all French or Norman names recorded in the Domesday Book as tenants-in-chief, sub-tenants or land holders took part in the Battle of Hastings. From Cahaignes or Cahagnes, Normandy, William de Cahaignes buckled on his armour, ready for the fray. Today we know his descendants as **Caines** or **Kaines**. Falaise in Normandy was the birthplace of William the Conqueror. William de Faleise received lands in return for his part in the battle. Today the surname is spelt **Fallas**. Hunfridus de Cuelai received lands in Norfolk for his part in the battle. He came from Cully-le-Patry. Today we know the surname as **Kewley** or **Cully**. From Vernon in the Eure valley came the family of that name headed by Richard de Vernon who after the rigours of the battle was awarded lands in Cheshire. This warrior was the first of the **Vernon** and **Varnon** families. Robert de Buci left his native Bouce to take part in the battle, in which he was one of the less important warriors. He became an under-tenant in Northamptonshire. William **Bussy** lived in Essex in 1310; by that time the family had become Anglo-French.

More than a hundred miles south-west of Paris is the ancient town of Tours. From here Picoth de Tour travelled to Lincolnshire, taking his birthplace as his name. Now we know the surname as **Towers** or **Tours**. Centuries later Huguenots fled from this same town and settled in Canterbury in Kent. Hugo de Angiers who resided in Worcester in 1208 hailed from Angiers. His descendants bear the surname **Angers** or **Aungiers**. The French place name Fay has given us a surname which has remained unchanged to this day. Margaret Le **Fay** was mentioned in the Surrey Subsidy Rolls for 1332.

It was more than a hop across the Channel for the **Gascoigne** family who originated in Gascony in south-west France. An early member of the family was William Le Gascun, a citizen of York in 1208. There are at least twelve variations of the surname, including **Gascoyne** and **Gaskins**.

It may appear that the surname **Eagle** or **Eagell** originated as a nickname from the bird of prey. However, a considerable number of people acquired the surname from their home town of l'Aigle in Normandy. Richer Del Egle resided in Northamptonshire in 1210. Perhaps a few holders of the surname **Fountain** or **Fontaine** had ancestors who dwelt by a spring or river, but many originated from the French town of Fontaine. The **Ivy** family owe their name to the ancestor who arrived at the end of the eleventh century from Ivoy. Geoffry de Ivoi was mentioned in the Oxfordshire Pipe Rolls for 1161.

La Hague in Normandy was the birthplace of the **Haig** family who arrived in the early twelfth century. One branch of the family settled in Bemersyde near Melrose in Scotland. Richard de Luci who lived in Bury St Edmunds acquired his surname from the family home town of Luc in Normandy. It has changed little, now spelt **Lucy**.

Nothing to do with one's behaviour, the surname **Manners** was given to families who originated from Mesnières. The surname **Licence** has nothing to do with legal documents. The family first came from Lison in Normandy shortly after the Norman Conquest. Godfrey De Lisun was mentioned in the Somerset Pipe Rolls for 1195. Other variations of the surname include **Lysons** and **Lison**.

The town of Mayenne is in the province of Maine which, with its regional capital Le Mans, was an important part of Norman territory. Several families from this region arrived in England at the end of the eleventh century. Among them was John Mayne of Berkshire. There are several versions of the modern surname, including **Mayne**, **Maine** and **Mains**.

One of the late French arrivals was the **Paveley** or **Pawley** family. Arriving some years after the Conquest, their original home was Pavilly, a small hamlet between Rouen and the coast. The **Artis** family owe their name to Artois, a small town in northern France which gave its name to artesian wells (the first European examples were sunk here in 1126). Robert Artis resided in Suffolk in 1327.

Beamish or **Beames** originated from Beaumais-sur-Dive in Normandy. One early member of the family was William de Beaumis, resident in Lincolnshire in 1192. A similar surname, **Bevill** or **Beavill**, stemmed from Beuville in Normandy. Robert de Beyville was a citizen of Huntingdon in 1225.

The small settlement of Aumale near Rouen was the birthplace of one family who came over with William. The warrior who assisted at the battle was Robert de Alba de Albemarle, who for his services received land in Devon. Little more than a century later the family had acquired more land in Dorset and Hampshire. The manor of Hinton, Hampshire, was owned by Reginald de Albamara in 1242 and later the name was changed to Hinton Admiral. Today we know the surname as **Damerell**, **Damiral** or **Damrell**.

One very influential Norman family came from either St Martin d'Aubigny or Aubigny. Nigel de Albengi who fought at the Battle of Hastings must have put up a terrific show as he was awarded lands in Bedfordshire, Berkshire and Buckinghamshire. There are several versions of the surname, including **Daubney**, **Dobney** and **D'Aubney**.

Also present at Hastings were Hugo de Widville, from Gouville, and Ralp de Mortemer. Widville's reward was land in Lincolnshire. Today we know his descendants as **Wyville**. The Mortemer family, headed by Peter Mortemer, owned land in Sussex in 1296. Today we have the surname **Mortimer** or **Murtimer**. Another who fought at that historic battle was Ralp De Nevilla who acquired his surname from his original home in Neville, Normandy. For his services he was given lands in various parts of the country, including Lincolnshire and Worcestershire. One of the oldest branches of the family are the **Nevills** who reside in Raby Castle, Durham. Some branches of the family use the surname **Newill**.

In the early twelfth century several families left Champagne for England. By 1195 Peter de Champaigne had settled in Lincolnshire. There are several versions of the surname, including **Champain**, **Champness** and **Champney**.

Although most of the French who came to England in the eleventh and twelfth centuries were from Normandy or Brittany a few families came from more distant parts of France. Reiner de Valene, mentioned in the City of London records for 1158, came from Valence, a town south of Lyons. In the thirteenth century the Valiance family founded a chapel and leper hospital on a site just outside Gravesend, Kent. Among the variations of the surname today we find **Vallance**, **Valence** and **Vallans**. The surname **Lyon** has remained the same since the family first arrived in England from Lyons. One of the first records was Lyon, son of Lyon, mentioned in the Somerset Assize Roll in 1293.

Surnames of family relationship

Surnames of relationship are commonly known as patronymics, a term which strictly speaking applies to surnames derived from a father's name although many modern surnames descended from the names of women and other family members. A study of the history of these surnames reveals the sense of family unity and affection, especially the strong bond between husband and wife in medieval England. The notion of family responsibility had been cultivated in earlier years by the Anglo-Saxons who had introduced laws to protect wives, widows and children. A number of surnames in this group originated from pet forms of female names, and many give good examples of the rhyming slang used so often by our medieval ancestors. This group of surnames allows us to build up a picture of domestic life over seven centuries ago.

The transition from pet name to surname was more gradual than that from other sources, and it is often harder to pick out very early examples. Many of the surnames in this group originated from Christian names which have fallen out of fashion – a pity, as the Anglo-Saxon language can be very descriptive and pleasant to the ear.

Adam, the first man on earth and the first forename, is an ancient Hebrew name meaning red earth or simply man. Many men were called Adam; their sons adopted it, or variations of it, as their surname. **Adkins** and **Atkins** were first used as pet names, for example John Adekynes of Warwickshire. There is a similar origin for **Adnett**, first spelt as Adynet.

Haldane was the result of a mixed marriage. Found mainly in the eastern counties, it comes from the Anglo-Scandinavian *healfdene*, meaning half Dane, and was given to the son of an English mother and Scandinavian father. Both **Bettis** and **Betts** stem from son of Beta, a pet form of Beatrice, an Italian name meaning 'making happy'. **Ansteys** derived from Anastasia, a Greek name meaning 'who shall rise again'. Teutonic Mahtildis was a forename meaning princess or noble lady; the Normans introduced it as Matilda. This led to the surnames **Maud**, **Mahood**, **Malt** and **Mold**, all started by men whose mother's name was Matilda. The fact that William the Conqueror's wife was called Matilda no doubt helped make it so popular.

Maw, **Maufe** and **Muffett** are a trio of names derived from Old English *mage*, meaning relative. Later the term *maugh* was used to describe a relative by birth or marriage: 'Maugh Husbondays syster or wyfs systyr or systyr in law'. Emma was responsible for the surnames

Emney and **Emm**, introduced by the Normans. It was a Latin name meaning nurse or caretaker. It went out of fashion with the medieval English but came into its own again some centuries later. **Emmerson**, similar in spelling but with a different meaning, was derived from the German *amalric*, meaning work rule. A beautiful sister or mother accounts for both **Fairbrother** and **Farson**, the brother or son of 'the fair one', a pet name often given to a beautiful woman. Our Anglo-Saxon ancestors used the word *foda* for one who had to be fed, sometimes a pet name for the youngest offspring. Today it has grown into the surnames **Foad**, **Foat** and **Food**. Elfred Fode of Norfolk was a youngest son

Even today **Babbs** is still used as a pet name for Barbara. Nicholas Babelot of Cornwall adopted the surname from his mother's pet name; later it was shortened, giving today's spelling. Barbara is a Greek name meaning strange or foreign and was usually given to a foreign-born wife of a local leader or prince. Hann was the Flemish form of John, a very popular Christian name in Yorkshire in the thirteenth century. A son whose father possessed this name was known as **Hanson**. Another origin for this surname stemmed from Rann, a shortened version of Randolph which was rhymed to Hann. Still used both as a Christian and surname, **Harold** achieved immortal fame at Hastings. It was in common use long before the Norman Conquest, introduced by the Vikings as *Haraldr*, meaning 'army power'.

Many people will be surprised to learn that the name of **Knott** or **Knottson** is closely connected with the celebrated King Canute. The Vikings introduced into England a personal name *Knutr*, later spelt *Knut*, the original pronunciation of Canute. This personal name was popular in East Anglia, the Fen country and Yorkshire.

Sibyl, meaning wise woman, was a popular Greek name among medieval maidens. William Sibeli who lived in Huntingdon in 1279 took his mother's Christian name as his surname. Today we know it as **Sibley**. Both **Mich** and **Mitchell** derive from Michael, a Christian name inherited from Hebrew, meaning 'who is like God'. Even today people named Mitchell are likely to be dubbed 'Mich'.

The celebrated Charlemagne had a daughter named Melisenda, taken from the Teutonic *Amalasuintha*, meaning 'work strong'. The French introduced it into England about 1200, when it was known as Milesindis. It gradually changed to **Millicent**, now used as both forename and surname. Centuries earlier the Greeks had the name Millicent for a girl, meaning song, but we have no record of it in England before the French version.

The French name *Bele* was a compliment. It meant beautiful, and medieval menfolk used it as a forename and a pet name. Alexander filius Bele adopted his mother's name. Today the surname has lost much of its glamour: we know it as **Beal**. The Greek Katherine or Catherine described a woman who was pure; it became one of the most popular female forenames in Europe. Abbreviated to Kati, Kitty and Katie, it was adopted by various sons as surnames such as **Kates** and **Katin**.

Another Old English slang phrase still in use today is *kidder*, meaning a man or boy. Our ancestors first coined it as Kitt, a pet form of Christopher, which in time became the surname **Kidd** or **Kidson**. Benedictus filius Sarre took his mother's name Sarah for his surname. Sarah originated from a Hebrew word meaning princess, and was responsible for the surnames **Sarah**, **Sara**, **Sare**, **Sarra** and **Sarre**. Not so well known was the Latin *Sabina*, but Sabrina, which was English, was used more widely. Both these led to the surname **Sablin**. Common in medieval records was the personal name **Sayer**, first introduced by the Normans as *Sigiheri*.

Who would think that **Pott** and **Potkin** were both developed from the little darling of the family? Philipot was a term meaning 'little Philip', and this in turn became Pot. Philip, a Greek name meaning 'lover of horses', was very popular until King Philip of Spain led the Spanish Armada in 1588, after which the name fell into disuse for some time. There must be many husbands and lovers who refer to their loved ones as 'Precious'. It was a medieval female Christian name and a form of endearment used by husbands coined from the Latin *preciosa,* meaning of great value. Though rare now as a Christian name, **Precious** is used as a surname. Another Latin female name still in use some eight centuries later, both as a Christian name and a surname, is **Prudence**. Robertus filius Prudence lived in Surrey in 1206.

The forename Nicholas was so popular it had at least thirty-five variations as a surname such as **Nicholls**, **Nicklass**, **Nicholas** and **Nixon**. Nicholas is a Greek name meaning 'victory people'. The feminine of the name was Nichola in English and Nicole in French, while one pet form was Nick. Sons and daughters acquired the surname from fathers and mothers, and other people acquired it from pet forms of the name. John Nicholls who lived in Oxford in 1697 was called Nick so often that he adopted it as his surname and became known as John Nicks.

If your name is **Hastings** your ancestors could have been born in that town. It is also possible they were Hasting, son of Hastang, a famous Anglo-Saxon chief. **Henn** has nothing to do with chickens; it was a pet name for Henrietta, the feminine form of Henry.

Godwin, an Old English forename meaning friend, was often shortened to *Gode*; this led to the word *godson*, meaning the best friend of the newly born son. From this developed the surnames **Godson** and **Goodson**. In 1366 the godson of an important City of London official, adopted his godfather's name as his surname and was known as Gilbert Goodchilde. The name is now known as **Goodchild**. Though not common, **Gabriel** as a Christian name was found mostly in Sussex. It came from a Hebrew word meaning 'hero of God', often referred to as the 'messenger'. **Garrison** has nothing to do with military establishments; it stemmed from 'son of Gerard', a Teutonic name meaning 'arm spear'.

One of the few English surnames to contain the letter Z is **Ozanne**, taken from the Hebrew *Ossanna*, meaning 'save now'. It was Latinised as *Hosanna*, a term used in religious songs, but the English preferred to use *Osanna* for the Christian name. *Ivo* was French for archer, and *Iva* was the feminine version which enjoyed some popularity in medieval England. This led to the surnames **Ivatt** and **Iveson**, both derived from *Iva*.

The trio of **Benn**, **Benson** and **Bennett** are all derived from the Christian name Bennett, originating from the Latin *Benedictus*, meaning blessed, a very favoured forename in the twelfth century. Even today those with the name Cecily or Cecilia find themselves called 'Ciss'. This habit is over seven centuries old, and a son whose mother was named Cecilia might adopt her pet name for his own surname and become known as **Sisson**. One that speaks for itself is **Brownson** – the son of a man called Brown, not as common as one would think, judging by the number of Browns that are about. **Kinsman** stemmed from medieval English *kinnes,* meaning a relative by blood, but later the term applied to a relative by marriage. John Cunesmon who lived in Worcester in 1275 was given the name because he lived a few miles away from a large group of his family.

Kitson and **Kitts** both have romantic beginnings. At one time it was the custom for a married couple named Christopher and Katherine to adopt jointly the pet name *Kytte*, which gave rise to the surnames. Another twinning of the wife's and husband's forenames led to the surname **Ibbetson**. Isabel was shortened to *Ibb*, and *Bot* was short for Hilbert; together they were known as *Ibbo*, and 'son of *Ibbo*' created the surname. This also accounted for the surname **Ibbs**.

While **Denison** originated from 'son of Denis', the name of several saints, or from the feminine form Denise, the surname **Denson** simply means the son of the dean. **Dodson** started out as 'son of Dodge', a pet name for Roger, based on the rhyming of Rodge and Dodge; while **Hodson** was the son of *Odo*, a name introduced by the Normans. It became a ritual for returning Crusaders to bring home with them water from the river Jordan to be used for the baptism of their children. In many cases, children baptised thus were named **Jordan**, at first a widely used Christian name and later a surname.

At one time William was the most fashionable name in England; the

Conqueror himself introduced it. It was a Norse name meaning helmet, and it attracted many pet forms and shortened versions. **Wilcock** and **Wilcox** were both based on a version, while **Wilkinson** was 'son of Wilkin', from the shortened Will. Also from Will we have **Wilson**. Will was probably the most popular of all English pet names.

Among the Teutonic names introduced into England in the twelfth century was *Lambert*, meaning 'bright land'. This was soon shortened to Lamb, and the son of Lamb became known as **Lampson**. Always more popular in the north, Andrew had many pet forms including Dan and Dand, the origin of the surname **Danson**. The Normans introduced Richard, a Christian name that originated in Germany meaning 'stern king', or powerful and brave. It soon gained favour, and Richard the Lion Heart boosted its popularity even further. With so many men bearing this Christian name, pet and shortened forms were numerous. Hickin or Higgin were two examples; these led to **Higginson**. Rick, a variation of Ricard, led to **Rick**, **Rix**, **Rixon** and **Riche**. We also have **Richardson** itself, spelt in many ways; even as late as 1683 there is an example of a George Richison.

Another name that has stood the test of centuries and is still in use today is Larry, short for Laurence. There was a feminine form too – Laurencia, so the surname **Larrett** could have stemmed from either father or mother. The Anglo-Saxons used the word *laessa* for the younger or smaller brother or child in the family. This evolved into the surnames **Lass** or **Less**. Not so well known was the girl's name Lettice taken from the Latin *Laetitia*, meaning happiness or joy. This too was cut down to **Lett**, the same as today's surname. The women's names Adelina, Emelina and Lecilina all led to **Lines** and **Lynes**.

One unusual Hebrew Christian name was Job; it meant the hated or persecuted one, and was a frequent character in medieval plays. Any son who inherited this name was soon known as **Jobson**.

Wat, a common pet name for Walter, coupled with Old Norman *magr*, meaning brother-in-law, together gave us the surname **Watmough**. Later, *magr* became *mough*, and described any relative, male or female. The surname **Christian** had no direct connection with the church; it was derived from Christian, a name for both males and females, and Christine, another feminine version of the forename. The name Claire in French, Clara in Latin, originally meant bright or fair, and today **Clare** is used both as a Christian name and a surname. Robertus Filius Clarae lived in Huntingdon in 1210. There is not much mystery about **Clarkson**: it simply meant the son of the clerk or cleric. **Coleson** and **Collinson** were derived from Coll, a pet name for Nicholas, though some with the name Coleson, especially if they live in East Anglia, may have inherited it from Old Danish *Kol*, a Scandinavian forename.

One of the oldest Old English Christian names was Cuthbert, first known as *Cudbeald*, meaning 'well-known splendour'. Our ancestors soon cut this short to *Cutt*, giving us the surname **Cutting**. Though at first sight **Lott** would appear to be a biblical name, it was in fact derived from Lota, a pet name from Allot, Amelot or Gillota, all women's names. The surname **Liley** though derived from a woman's name, does not come from Lily, but from Lylie, a pet form of Elizabeth.

Jack was the most common pet form of John, derived from Jankin. By the thirteenth century, when John became popular, other pet forms were introduced – Jan, Jake and Johan. From all these stemmed the surname **Jackson**. In medieval England, Jack was the general term to describe a man or boy, the same as *Jacques* was the common expression to describe a French peasant. Contrary to public opinion, Jacob, Hebrew for supplanter, was not a Jewish forename; it was used in England before the Norman invasion. From Jacob sprang the surnames **Jacobson**, **Jacoby** and **Jacobi**.

Ancestors of those named **Graveson** had nothing to do with grave diggers but obtained the name from son of the *greyve* (a steward) or from the Old Norman personal name *Grefi*, meaning a count or earl. At one time this surname was found mainly in Yorkshire, in the Leeds area. **Hobson** started out as the son of Hobb, a pet name rhymed on Rob, short for Robert. **Uncle** and **Ungles**, though derived from the French *oncle,* were not family surnames. Uncle stemmed from Anglo-Scandinavian *Ulfketel*, a personal name meaning 'wolf kettle', found mostly in Suffolk, Yorkshire and Lincolnshire.

The Anglo-Saxons and Scandinavians were fond of legends which were passed down from one generation to the next. The Old English personal name *Wada* was taken from the legend of Wade, a sea giant dreaded and honoured by tribes living on the coast of the North Sea and Baltic. This legend still lives on in the surnames **Wade** and **Wadeson**. Anglo-Scandinavians were responsible for **Tuck**, derived from the Old Danish *Tuki*, a personal name common in Lincolnshire and Norfolk.

Old English *treowe* and *lufu* were combined to give **Truelove**, a pet name meaning faithful love. John Trulove who lived in 1384 acquired his surname from his mother who had been given this pet name by her admiring husband. **Tomkinson** started as 'son of Tomkin', a pet name meaning Little Tom; William Tomkynes who lived in 1300 was one of the first men to adopt it as a surname. **Margetts** was derived from 'son of Margaret', a popular Greek name in medieval times meaning pearl. There is a record of John Margaret, son of Merget, Suffolk, 1460.

Maeve was the legendary queen of Ireland, who became the Fairy Queen Mab. From this developed the Celtic feminine forename of

Mabel – the Queen of Mirth. It was not long before young women with this name were addressed as Mab or Mabs, and it was only natural that men whose mother bore this name found themselves called **Mabey**, **Mabon** or **Mabbs**. These surnames should not be confused with **Maul** or **Malkinson**, derived from Mall, a pet form of Mary, one of the oldest and most consistently popular of all women's names. It came from the Hebrew meaning 'bitter water' and the name symbolised the sea of life.

A thirteenth-century pet name for women and men was **Tibbs**, derived from Isabel or Tibald, short for the Greek name Theobald, meaning 'people's prince'. In a similar vein, **Tillett** stemmed from Till, the pet form of Matilda; in the Yorkshire Poll Tax returns for 1379 there is a record of one 'Tillot – Housewyfe'.

In order to distinguish son from father, the Normans added Fitz to names, so Hugh became **Fitzhugh** and later **Fithie**. Few early records list Fitz as a Christian name though it was given on occasions. Teutonic *Fulcard* was a forename meaning 'brave people'; it eventually led to **Folkson** and **Foxen**. **Frearson** was taken from the French *frère* and simply means 'son of the friar'. **Lowson** had two origins, either the son of *Low*, a pet name for Laurence, or the son of the wolf. The same is true of **Luff**: it was taken from Old English *leof*, meaning beloved, resulting in the Christian name *Lufa*, or derived from *louve*, the feminine of wolf.

Among the terms of affection that later became surnames we find Old English *mulling*, meaning darling. **Mullings** and **Mowling** both derive from this source, and William Molling who lived in the City of London in 1313 was the son of Mullying – his mother. **Nelson** is exactly what it says – the son of Nell, taken from the Gaelic *Niall*, meaning the champion. In Yorkshire, however, the surname is nearly always **Nell**. Another easy one is **Gibson**, the son of Gibb, a pet name for Gilbert, while **Gipson** stemmed from Gip, another pet name for Gilbert, a German name signifying 'bright pledge'.

Gepp was taken from Geoffrey, a Christian name introduced by the Anglo-Saxons meaning 'the pledge of peace'. **Gillian** and **Gillan** stem from a name used by both male and females – Julian and Juliana, Latin for 'the one with soft hair'. **Abel** and **Ablett** originated from Abel which, though primarily a boy's name, was on occasions given to girls. It was borrowed from Hebrew and it meant the breath of God. Even today Philip often finds his name cut to Phil; when our ancestors did it they made the surname **Fill**. With almost the same pronunciation **Fayle** has an entirely different meaning; it was Manx as in *Mac Giolla Phoil*, the son of Paul's servant.

Thomas is nearly always referred to as Tom, a habit that has been with us for centuries and responsible for **Thom** and **Thompson**. A much later version of this surname was **Thompsett**; the earliest record we can find is 1792. **Tapping** was from the son of *Taeppa*, an Anglo-Saxon chief who ruled an area now covered by Berkshire and Buckinghamshire. It is thought another Saxon chief of this name lived in Kent. **Stoffer** was a pet name for Christopher, rhymed on the last syllables of the name; the surname was rare in medieval records, but there was a Giles Stoffer who lived in 1568.

Petronilla, a name favoured by medieval maidens, was taken from a saint reputed to be the daughter of St Peter; from it sprang the surname **Parnall**. The son of Patrick led to **Pateman**, while **Pavey** originated from *Pavia*, a French female name meaning peach. Jeff, short for *Galfridus*, a popular name among peasants, was responsible for **Geffen** and **Jeff**, but **Gem** was taken from the Italian *Gemma*, a jewel. Though in Central Europe the name Wenceslas was popular, the Anglo-Saxons preferred their version – Stephen. It came from the Greek for crown and was soon used as a surname in the form of **Stephenson** or **Stimpson**. From Duning, son of Dun – the dark one, we get **Downing**, and **Dudding** son of Dudd – the short fat man.

Edmund – the defender of property – gave us **Edmonson**. **Elcock** had two sources: son of Elias, or Ellis, a pet name for Elizabeth; **Elkin** came from the same source. **Ead** derived from Eda, a pet name for Edith, known as *Eadgyo* to the Anglo-Saxons. **Edds** stemmed from Edwina, one of the oldest female names known in England as does **Edkins**.

Some pet names evolved from what were already pet names. A good example is the pet name Ibb from Isabel. This was again changed, resulting in Ebbot and Ebbet and Ebb. From these sprang the surnames **Ebbs**, **Ebbetts**, **Ebbitt** and **Ebutt**. 'Son of the master' resulted in **Masterson**, and John Maisterson, freeman of York in 1323, was originally apprenticed to his own father. The Christian name Matthew was responsible for a considerable number of surnames. **Masset** stemmed from Masse, a feminine form of Matthew, **Mathes** and **Mathesson** were derived from Mathi, a pet form, and **Mayhew** resulted from the French pronunciation of the Christian name.

Batt was a common abbreviation for Bartholomew and gave us **Bateson** and **Batten**, two early surnames; a Walter Batun lived in Essex in 1148. **Perkin** and **Parkin** started out as *Per* (Peter) and *kin* (little) – Little Peter was a popular pet name among peasants. Maud and Walter Parkynes are mentioned in 1332; his father was known locally as Little Peter.

Gavin started out as a Christian name: it was the Scottish form of the English *Gawayne* and French *Gauvain*, King Arthur's nephew. Gavin, meaning 'hawk of the plains', was little used until the Bretons introduced it into East Anglia, where it soon gained favour.

Child was taken from the Old English *cild,* usually given to the youngest of the family or one who was a minor at the time of his parents' death. **Cass** was a pet name for Cassandra, also responsible for **Casson. Cain** can be misleading: it had nothing to do with the biblical name but derived from *Keina*, short form of Welsh female names such as *Ceindrych*, or *Ceinwen*, 'the beautiful one'.

From Lincolnshire, original home of the first Danish settlers, we get **Roulson**, son of Rolf, and in Cumbria the Teutonic name *Ralf*, meaning 'house wolf', started the surname **Rawlinson**. In a similar vein, the Normans introduced *Reinald*, meaning 'mighty counsel', with the resultant surname **Reynoldson**. The surnames **Robertson, Robeson** and **Robins** all mean son of Robert, which was first spelt *Rodbert*, French fashion. Introduced by the later Normans, and meaning 'bright fame', it became one of our best loved Christian names.

Hick was a pet name for Richard, in common use in medieval England. Robert Hichmughe, residing in Oxford in 1584, acquired his surname through a family relationship; it meant the brother-in-law of Hich. This led to the modern surnames **Hitchmough** and **Hickmott**. Other branches of the family who derived their surname from this pet name are **Hitch**, **Hytch** and **Hitches**. Stephen Hichie was a citizen of Norwich in 1300.

A popular first name from the twelfth century was Laurence, taken from the Latin. It was not long before the English abbreviated it to Law. This pet name soon became a surname – **Law**, **Lawes** and **Laws**. When this surname was passed on to the eldest son it became **Lawson**. One such member of the family was Richard Lawisson, living in Cornwall in 1327.

The Anglo-Saxons used the pet name *Hudd* in place of Hugh. This led to the surname **Hudd**. William Hudde was mentioned in the York Pipe Rolls for 1210. Hudd's brother-in-law became **Hudsmith**; Ralph Hudsmyth was a Guild Merchant of Preston in 1582. The son of Hudd was known as **Hudson**.

There is little doubt about the origins of **Johnson**. It is only natural that today it is one of the most common English surnames as John was the most popular forename in the thirteenth century. From the multitude of people to hold the surname in those early days we find John Jonessone who dwelt in Surrey in 1287. We also get Jan from John, hence the surname **Janson**. The pet name Janekyn was given to the youngest John in the family. Richard Janekyn of Sussex, 1296, was one of the first members of the **Jenkins** family.

From *Elias*, the Greek form of the Hebrew *Elijah*, the English used Elis as a first name. This was then passed on as a surname. John Elys, resident in Cumbria in 1318, was the son of Elias de Bampton. Rather than take on his father's surname (taken from Bampton, a small hamlet in the Lake District), he adopted his father's first name. There are several ways of spelling the surname, including **Ellis**, **Elias** and **Heelis**.

The French name *Alain*, or the Breton *Alun*, was the name of a Welsh and Breton saint. When the Bretons settled in Lincolnshire it became very popular as a first name, with at least eleven variations of it developing as a surname, including **Allon**, **Alleyn** and the more common **Allen**. One of the early Lincolnshire families was that of Geoffrey Alein who resided in the county in 1234.

There are at least ten variations of the surname **Halliday** or **Holloday**. They all stem from Old English *haligdaeg*, a holy day or religious festival. Those families fortunate enough to have a child born on such a day might give them this name. Reginald Halidei, residing in Bedford in 1171, was one such child.

The personal name John is spelt differently in many European countries. The Flemish form of the name was *Hann*, which found its way into England. Later, medieval slang *coc* was added to the name. This resulted in the surname **Hancock**. Among Shropshire records we find Thomas Hancoc, 1274.

Old English *leofdaeg* meant a special day or 'dearday'. Apart from birthdays or other family anniversaries it was also a special day appointed for a meeting between litigants with the purpose of settling disputes. It became a common Christian name in medieval England and later a surname that we know today as **Loveday** or **Lowday**. Robert Luvedey, living in Kent in 1200, must have been born on such a day.

The popular Norman first name *Roland* was introduced at the time of the Norman Conquest. It was the name of one of Charlemagne's followers. The son soon became known as **Rowlandson** and the name was at first common in Cumbria, for example William Roulandman, 1332. Just across the border in north Lancashire the name was more commonly **Roulson** or **Ronson**.

The Scandinavian *Rannulfr*, meaning 'shield wolf', was introduced into England by the Normans and changed to Randolph. This in turn was shortened as a pet name to Rand which ended up as another pet name, Rand-el. Thomas Randel was recorded in the Suffolk Feet of Fines for 1250. From these sources has sprung the surnames **Randall**, **Randle** and **Randoll**. The full forename became a surname also, today known as **Randolph**. One example was Robert Randolph of Cornwall, 1260.

The French word *paien*, from the Latin *paganus*, referred to a villager or rustic. Later, it meant a heathen or one of no faith. The name was given to children whose baptism had been delayed, or to parents whose religious zeal was not as fervent as it should have been. By the twelfth century it was given as a name without any thought of its original meaning. It has resulted in at least fourteen surnames, including **Paine**, **Payen**, **Pagan** and **Paynes**. One famous holder of the name was Thomas Paine, the English writer who supported the American rebels in the War of Independence.

From the French *pentecost*, we get the first name given to a child born on that festival day. Pentecoste de Wendleswurda, resident in Surrey in 1187, must have been born then. From that name the surnames **Pankhurst** and **Pentecost** have evolved. There is no doubt about the origins of **Noel** or **Nowell**. It was given by delighted parents to a baby born at Christmas. William Nowell of Huntingdon, 1248, was probably a Christmas baby. *Pâque*, the forerunner of today's **Pack**, **Pakes** and **Paik**, was Old French for Easter, given to a child born during this religious festival. John Pac resided in Bury St Edmunds in Suffolk in 1190. The surnames **Whitson** and **Whitsun** have no connection with that festival: they derive from the 'son of White or Whitt'.

Geneviève was the patron saint of Paris. The pet name became **Geeves** followed by **Geaves** and **Jeeves**. Both **Dixon** and **Dickson** are easy: they originate from 'the son of Dick'. Robert Dixson was a London merchant in 1429. Children with the name of Robert often had their name cut to Rob, then rhymed to Nob. This resulted in the surnames **Nobbs** and **Nopps**.

The Old English personal name *Aeoelheard*, meaning 'noble hard', was popular long before the Norman invasion. It resulted in the surnames **Ellard**, **Adlard** and **Hallard**. In the Domesday Book there is an *Ailarus* who held lands in Sussex. Another Old English first name, *Aeoelric*, resulted in the surnames **Allwright** and **Oldwright**.

Some children with the first name of Julian or Juliana were given the pet name Jull. This evolved into the surnames **Jull** or **Jolles.** Old French *bel-fiz* meant dear son and was often used as a term of affection. There is an Odo Belfiz of Hampshire, 1176. The name today is **Beavis** and **Bovis**.

The Old English pet name *maide-kin*, meaning little maid, was usually given to the youngest daughter as a term of endearment. Centuries later, the descendants of these young women are known as **Makin**, **Meakin** or **Meekins**. Another pet name for a favourite daughter was the nickname Emmot for Emma. When the mother's pet name became a surname, it resulted in **Emmett** and **Hemmett**.

The Germans had a first name *Hamon* which the French changed to *Hamond* and brought to England with the Norman invasion. One member of the family was Willelmus filius Haymundi who resided in Surrey in 1221. It is the origin of the surnames **Hammond**, **Hammon**, and **Hammant**.

Valentine was the name of a third-century Roman saint. It became popular as a first name in the twelfth century, then adopted as a surname. Today it has become **Valentine** and **Vallintine**.

Piers was the French version of Peter. It was widely used in medieval England and resulted in at least sixteen surnames. One example was Gilbert Perse, a London merchant at the end of the twelfth century. It has changed little since then, known today as **Pierce**, **Piers** or **Perse**. John Piersson of Warwickshire, 1332, took his father's name as his surname, which we know today as **Person**. John Person was a London doctor who qualified in 1559.

An unusual woman's name was *Aldus* which, taken by sons, became **Aldous** or **Aldis**. Peter Aldous was mentioned in the Suffolk Subsidy Rolls for 1327.

A personal name that became a surname and remained unchanged for nearly a thousand years is **Utting**. The family was well established in Boldon, Durham, over nine centuries ago. **Rogers** and **Rodgers** are family names that originated from the personal name Roger, introduced by the Normans and meaning 'fame spear'. It appears in the Essex division of the Domesday Book with an entry for Rogerus. George Rogers, a citizen of Dartford, Kent, qualified as a doctor in 1609.

Old English *Wende* meant the dweller by the bend. The surname **Wend** was probably changed to the pet name Wendy for a female member of the family. This in turn became the surname **Wendy**. Thomas Wendy from Cambridge became a doctor in 1527 and was the personal physician to King Henry VIII.

Old English, French or Scandinavian?

British surnames originate from such a bewildering variety of sources that even experts are puzzled by some of them. Add to this the fact that they can be English, French, Scandinavian, Latin or Hebrew in language and origin and we have a vast subject that still requires a great deal of research. Many people are curious about the meaning of their name and even more so about its original nationality. A question frequently asked is 'Is it Old English, French or Scandinavian?'

The surname **Thorp** derived from one of the many place names Thorpe (there are at least twenty-two in England) or from residence in a hamlet or outlying dairy farm. All these stem from Old English *thorp*. But **Tovey**, although it sounds very similar, was derived from the Norman *tofi* and the Danish *tovi*, meaning 'nation ruler'. In the early days the surname was found chiefly in East Anglia, where the Danes settled. King Canute's chief follower was known as Tovi the Proud.

St Alban, the first British martyr, gave rise to the forename Alba, which in turn became the surname **Alban**. This name has no connection with **Albin**, derived from the Latin *albus*, meaning white – the man with fair hair or complexion. The French gave us **Jardin** – one who worked or dwelt near a garden – and **Juster**, a man who took part in tournaments or jousts, a medieval pastime that enabled young inexperienced knights to learn the arts of war.

An interesting group of surnames is **Narracott**, **Narramore** and **Narraway**. They all originate from place names in Devon. William de Northcote lived in Narracott in 1330. Reginald Bynorthemore, the dweller north of the moor, lived in Narramore in 1318 while Nicholas Bynortheweye, the man who lived north of the road, lived in Narraway in 1333.

If your name is **Oxborough** the home of your ancestors was Oxborough in Norfolk; William de Oxeburg lived in the village in 1275. **Ostler**, **Hosteller** and **Horsler** are not only surnames, they tell the history of English hotels and inns. They derive from the French *hostelier*, a name given to a man who received lodgers or entertained guests. At first this business of putting up guests for the night was confined to monasteries, then traders opened inns. One early holder of the name was William Hostiler of Eynsham Abbey, Oxfordshire, who lived in 1190.

Pallister stemmed from the French *palis*, a maker of wooden palings or fences, a trade still carried on some thousand years later. Also from the French comes the surname **Parmenter**, meaning tailor, another trade that has changed little over the centuries. Hebrew *Pesakh* became French *Pasche* and eventually English *Paches* – Easter, and people born at Easter were known as **Pash**. A man unlucky enough to live in a rough enclosure was known as **Roffey**. Amri de la Rogheye lived in Roffey near Horsham, West Sussex, in 1275.

A common name in Lancashire and Yorkshire is **Schofield** – the man who lived by a field with a hut, while **Sizer** described a member of the Assize, one of the first being William Sisar of York in 1379. **Lacy**, mentioned in the Domesday Book, was a French family who arrived with William the Conqueror and lived in Lassy. One Yorkshire surname of Anglo-Saxon origin is **Aked**, from Old English *ac-heafod*, the dweller by the oak-covered headland, while **Ackroyd** meant a dweller by the oak clearing.

The Anglo-Saxons and Normans each had a different word meaning 'noble hard'. The English word was *aeolheard*, the Norman *adelard,* which was borrowed from the German. In both forms the word became a popular personal name and later a surname with several modern spellings, among them **Adlard**, **Allard** and **Hallett**.

Amand was derived from the Latin *amandus*, lovable, the name of four saints. It was used also in the feminine form and may have been confused with *Amanda*, a Greek name which means protection. The surname **Angel**, a nickname from the Latin *angelus,* messenger or saint, was probably given to messengers. The first record of the surname occurs in Kent with Warinus Angelus who lived in the county in 1193.

Our Anglo-Saxon ancestors had several words connected with the fairy folk and pixies. One word they used was *aelfweard*, meaning elf guard, mentioned in the Domesday Book as Aeluvard. Today the surnames from this quaint nickname are spelt **Allward** and **Ellward**. Another surname, **Alven**, comes from Old English *aelfwine*, meaning elf friend. In the early days of surnames it was found mostly in Kent and Sussex; Richard Elvene lived in Sussex in 1296. A rather touching personal name that first became a surname in Hertfordshire is **Bellmaine**, from the French *belle main*, beautiful hand. Who was the first adoring husband or lover to give this unusual pet name to his loved one? **Bewt** is simple enough: it derived from Old English *belt* (still in use) and described a maker of belts.

Richard Cagge who resided in Worcester in 1275 acquired his name through residence near the cage, a prison for petty malefactors. Other ancestors of the surname **Cage** may have helped build them or been employed as keepers. These tiny prisons were still used in the early nineteenth century. **Caddick** originated from the French *caduc*, meaning infirm, probably used as a nickname for a man who was unsteady on his feet. Do you have an artistic streak running through your family? The name **Image** was first given to a man who made images from wood or stone, a carver or sculptor.

Some surnames have more than one origin. The surname **Keats**, for example, was a nickname for a greedy, grasping individual as well as for a man who lived in an outhouse for sheep or cattle, usually a herdsman. The man who lived near, or worked at, a clay pit was known as **Lampitt**, while **Lang**, one of our older surnames, described a long tall man. Aetheric des Langa lived in Northumberland in AD 972.

A soldier armed with a crossbow was known as an arblaster, a nickname given also to men who made crossbows or paid their land rent by supplying their lord of the manor with crossbowmen. Today we know the surname as **Alabaster** or **Arlblaster**. Though **Bagge** originated from the Teutonic personal name *Bago*, it was the nickname given to a man who made or sold bags. **Baldwin**, another name that originated from a Teutonic personal name, meant bold friend, a personal name popular in England before and after the Norman Conquest.

Edricus de **Algate** lived close to Aldgate in the City of London in 1219. The Teutonic personal name *Anseheim*, meaning God's helmet, led to the surname **Ansell**, first recorded in Yorkshire. Part Saxon and part French, **Archer** described a bowman, while **Bannister** was derived from the French *banastre*, a basket maker. The man who lived near an enclosure for young trees was known as **Impey**, while **Jagger** was a West Riding name describing a carrier, carter or pedlar. John Jagher, who lived in York in 1379, is mentioned in local records as a carrier.

From Northumberland and Yorkshire came **Ingram**. This name originated from Old German *engle*, a raven. Anglo-French *saghe*, to saw, was the nickname given to a man employed in a sawpit; today we know it as **Sawyer**. The French *escriven*, to write, a nickname for one who wrote books and manuscripts, led to **Scriven**. The town beadle was always recognised by the staff of office that he carried. This led to nicknames connected with the way he carried or waved his staff, resulting in the surnames **Wagstaff** and **Waple** (wag-pole). Another important official was the town nightwatchman. His nickname was derived from the French *guaite*, giving us the surnames **Wait**, **Waites** and **Wates**. Roger le Wayte was the watchman of a Suffolk town in 1221.

Rivers and streams were important in medieval England. They supplied water for agriculture, food in the way of fish, and in many cases power through waterwheels. **Wear** was the name given to a man employed at a weir or dam used as a fish trap, while **Wheelhouse**, a West Yorkshire name, was given to the man in charge of the waterwheel. **Whetter** was the man who used the waterwheel to drive his stone to sharpen his knives and tools.

Though **Pedlar** could be a nickname for a hawker or pedlar, it also originated from the French *pied-de-lièvre*, meaning hare foot, given to a man who was fleet of foot, a speedy messenger. **Pilbeam**, a Sussex and west Kent surname, originated from a lost place of that name in Sussex. **Gammon** came from the Norman *gamb*, meaning little leg, and **Garnett** was the man in charge of the granary.

Waldef de Yuebanc lived in Cumbria in 1258 – the man who lived by the yew bank. Today his descendants are known as **Ewbank**. **Usher** is simple enough – a doorkeeper; usually an urban name, it was first found in places like Colchester and York. Vine-growing was an important occupation in the Middle Ages; a worker at the vineyard soon attracted the nickname **Vine**, also given to a man who sold wine. **Dingle** was given to the man who lived near a deep dell, while **Down**, from Old English *dun*, applied to a family living near the Downs in Kent and Sussex; one such family was represented by John atte Doun, who lived in Sussex in 1296.

The Anglo-Saxons had established towns and boroughs long before the arrival of the Normans. They were safe places for markets, places where money was minted, and centres of defence. These towns had officials, very similar to those employed in civic duties some thousand years later. The beadle or, to quote his Old English name, *bydel* was a man of some authority, mentioned in the Domesday Book with Brictmarus Bedel. This one official led to a multitude of surnames, including **Beadle**, **Beadell**, **Beedle**, **Biddle** and **Buddle**.

Dallman was the dweller in the dale. **Dempster** was an important man; his name derived from *deemer*, a judge. First used as a nickname for a kneader of bread, **Day** and **Dey** then referred to a dairy maid, and later became a general term for a female servant. Aluricus filius Faber was mentioned in the Domesday Book for Suffolk; his nickname came from the Latin **Faber**, meaning smith. **Fabian** was from the Latin *faba*, a bean. From the French *galopin* came **Galpin**, the nickname for a messenger but also used as a nickname for the boy who turned the spit in the kitchen. **Haggard** was the nickname for a wild or untamed boy.

A new arrival in the village became known as **Newman**. The families who lived near oak trees were known as **Oak**, **Noakes** or **Nokes**. The man who sifted corn was known as **Riddler**. The surname **Rainbow** had nothing to do with the weather; it originated from the Teutonic personal name *Reinbald* – 'bold might'. **Felix** had nothing to do with cats; it came from the Latin *felix*, happy. **Ferrier** was the ferry keeper. The nickname given to a cheat or impostor was **Fetters**.

Gaelic *naomhin*, little saint, gave us **Niven**. The French *passe-mer*, cross the sea, a nickname for a sailor, resulted in **Passmore**. Did you have any poachers in the family? One of the first poachers was known as **Pearcey**, from the French *pierce haie*, meaning 'pierce hedge'. **Hussey** was derived from the medieval *husewyf*, mistress of a family or wife of a householder, a complimentary term for women, unlike its modern equivalent.

From the Old English *mangere* developed **Monger**, the name for a trader or dealer, still used in the terms ironmonger and fishmonger. **Mewer** and **Mewes** have an interesting background. They derive from the French *mue*, a cage for hawks, usually the place where they were kept while moulting. The name was later used to describe stables (hence mews cottages, often made from converted outbuildings). The nickname first applied to men in charge of the hawk cages but was also given to men who lived in or near Meaux in Yorkshire. **Miles**, first recorded in the Domesday Book as Milo, was taken from the Latin *miles*, a soldier.

One of the Breton contingents who fought for William at Hastings was the **Talbot** family. Their name originated from *talebot*, lamp-black, a nickname for bandits who blacked their faces to avoid recognition. **Theaker** was first used mainly in East Anglia, from Old English *thekja*, to cover, a nickname given to men who roofed buildings. The men who covered the roofs with tiles were known as *tille-thekers*.

Most inns and hotels still pride themselves on their service. The surname **Service** originated from the French *cervoise*, meaning ale; it was used as a nickname for a seller of ale or an innkeeper. **Single** had nothing to do with the marital state of the holder; it stemmed from Old English *sengel*, the man who dwelt by the burnt clearing. Alan de la Single lived in Sussex in 1296. The name was common in this county because of the large amounts of forest land that were being cleared. From Suffolk and Essex we find **Slade**, the man who lived in the valley. In these flat counties, with few valleys, the name was especially outstanding. The Old Norman *skilamaor* led to today's **Skillman**, a nickname given to a man who was trustworthy, not skilled at his trade.

First mentioned in the Domesday Book as Ernui, from the Saxon *earnwig*, meaning 'eagle warrior', we now have the surname **Arneway**. **Bass** indicated a short, thickset man, and **Bates** was from a pet form of Bartholomew or a nickname for a boatman. From the Latin *travetarius* sprang the surname **Tranter**, a nickname for a carrier or hawker; Simon le Traunter who lived in Warwick in 1332 was listed as a carrier. **Unwin** from East Anglia was derived from Old English *hunwine*, young bear friend, a delightful title that implied strong friendship.

Have you ever watched workmen digging and ramming earth in the preparation of foundations? The medieval man who worked on excavations was known as a *tupant* while the huge hammers he used were known as *tuppis*. He was given the nickname of **Tupper**, and though we have now progressed to mechanical shovels and diggers men are still required for the final operations. A good old Yorkshire name is **Turnbull**, a nickname denoting strength or bravery. Legend has it that there was once a famous Yorkshire horse of that name renowned throughout England for his feats of strength.

Bevrege was a drink used to clinch a bargain; it was used as a nickname for a man who obtained free drinks for bargains he had no intention of keeping. The name has changed little over the centuries and today we spell it **Beveridge**. A fairly common name from the marshy areas that abounded along the banks of the lower Thames was **Binney** or **Binnie**, the dweller on the land enclosed by streams. **Byass** was the man who resided in the house in the bend of the road or track. Working at the hall or living by the shallow copse invited the nickname **Seal**, also given to a resident of Seal in Kent or Seale in Surrey.

There was as great a diversity of characters in medieval England as there is today. Men we would dub 'smooth' were nicknamed *smethe*, the polished one, leading to the surname **Smeed**. It should be added that the nickname was also given to the man who lived at the smooth, level place or who resided in Smeed, Kent. The active lad always full of spirits and darting about was known as **Snell**; the same lad may have been called **Spark**.

Stammers had nothing to do with a man's speech. The name originated from Old English *stanmaer*, 'stone fame', and most holders of this surname first came from East Anglia. A few families from Stanmore in Middlesex or Stanmer in Sussex acquired the same name. **Cavell** was from the French *chauve*, a nickname for a bald man. **Chalcroft** was the dweller by the calves' croft, and **Chalker** an occupational name for a white-washer but occasionally used of a man living near the Sussex or Kentish downs.

Chambre was French for a palace reception room where people came to pay their taxes, and the clerk who collected them was soon known as **Chambers**. Later the term applied to a servant or attendant, such as a chambermaid. Have you ever heard of a *flaunier*? It was a French custard or pancake, and the cook who made them was given the nickname **Flanner**. The surname **Kettle** has only remote connections with the household utensil of that name. The name originated from the Scandinavian *ketill*, a sacrificial cauldron, first mentioned in AD 972 with *Grym Kytel*. Men who lived on top of hills were usually known as **Knapp** or **Knowles**, names which were first used in Devon, Kent and Sussex. **Gunter** was a Teutonic personal name meaning 'battle army'.

There are several origins for **Hope**. The nickname was given to the man who lived in or near raised land in fen country, or a peasant who resided in a small enclosed valley, while some holders of the name came from Hope in Devon or Yorkshire. The servant at the house usually implied service at a religious house or convent and led to **House** or **Hows**. The tenant who occupied his own land was known as **Helder** and the original duties of a **Hayward** were to guard the enclosed lands ready for the production of hay. **Helm** was Old English for a covering or shelter; the nickname was given to the herdsman who looked after the roofed shelter for cattle. We have three surnames that described men with a quick temper: **Gear** was given to one with sudden fits of passion, **Geary** to a changeable, giddy person, and **Gerish** to the man with a reputation for being wild.

A surname with a more peaceful meaning is **Gossard**, from Old English *gos-hierde*, goose herd. **Pipe** was the musician who played the pipe, or it came from *Pypa*, a woman's name, or was the man who lived near the water pipe, conduit or aqueduct. **Ledger** had no connection with ancient book-keeping; it stemmed from the Teutonic personal name meaning 'people spear' and was very common on mainland Europe before arriving in England through the influence of St Leger, a seventh-century bishop.

There are two origins for **Lock**. The nickname was given to a man with curly locks or to one employed as a lock keeper. From the southern and western counties we find **Millward** and **Mullard** from Old English *myleweard*, one in charge of a mill.

Hathaway, a name famous for its association with Shakespeare, was originally Old English, from *headuwig*, the war warrior. The surname was at first most common in Herefordshire and Gloucestershire, and especially in Warwickshire, the home of Ann Hathaway, wife of William Shakespeare. **Halstead**, a surname that appeared in large numbers in Essex and Leicestershire, was derived from the man who worked at the hall buildings, usually outhouses away from the manor. The name also originated from one of the numerous places named Halstead.

A man who was a rower or employed as a galleyman was known as **Galley**. Also, galilee described a porch or chapel at the entrance to a church, more common in cities such as Durham and Ely where men with this name might be employed in the cathedrals. From the French historical romances stemmed the name **Bellinger**, a Teutonic personal name meaning 'bear spear' and the name of a famous French knight. It was the custom in medieval England to give a special cake for alms; later, godparents gave these cakes to their godchildren and **Ketchell** was derived from the men who made or sold these cakes.

The Old English personal name *Wigmund*, meaning 'war protection', originated from Old Danish and Swedish *Vimund*. From this grew the surnames **Wyman** and **Weyman**, which in the early days were confined to Lincolnshire and Norfolk. The man who lived on the headland facing out to sea was known as **Ness**.

The Old Danish name *Aggi* led to the modern surname **Agg**, while another Scandinavian personal name, *Auti*, resulted in the surname **Autt** or **Awty**. From Denmark or Normandy *Vidarr* or *Withar*, denoting dweller by the willow tree, evolved into today's surname **Wither**. John Wythiar resided in Sussex in 1327. One personal name with mixed origins was the Danish *Alger*, Old English *Aeoelar* and Norman *Alfgeirr*, from which we get the surnames **Alger** and **Elgar**. Irrespective of the origins, the surnames were first used in East Anglia and Yorkshire, where Scandinavian influence was greatest.

Leof, meaning dear or beloved, led to the surnames **Leaf**, **Leefe** and **Life**. Robert Levi, living in Worcester in 1275, acquired his surname from *Leofwig*, meaning beloved warrior. **Leavey** and **Lovie** are today's versions of that name. If your surname is **Bald** or **Bauld** it does not signify that your ancestors were 'thin on top'. It originated from the Old English personal name *Beald*. One example was John Balde, a resident of Lincoln in 1150. *Godhere* was a personal name meaning 'good army', usually bestowed on someone with military prowess. Today the surname is **Gooder** or **Gouda**. Used as a personal name and also a prefix in English place names, *Tat* or *Tata* was in common use even before the Norman Conquest. *Tata's halh* became Tattenhall, Tattenhoe or Tatenhill, suggesting that this was a popular personal name among Saxon chiefs. Richard Tate was a resident of Cornwall at the end of the thirteenth century, and the surname remains **Tate** to this day.

Norman and Danish *Farman*, a personal name in both languages, led to today's **Farman** and **Ferhor**. They were common names in Yorkshire; Richard Fareman lived in the county in 1260. Recorded in the Domesday Book, *Eadric*, an Old English personal name meaning prosperity, was written as *Edricus*. Robert Eadric resided in Oxford in 1221. The modern surname is **Edrich**.

Both **Haslock** and **Hasluck** originate from the Norman personal name *Aslaker*. One of the first to bear the name was Richard Hasloke, resident in Norwich in 1086.

A surname that has remained unchanged for over nine centuries is **Bade**, which was derived from Old English *Bada*. Bictricus Bade lived in Hampshire in 1066, the year of the Battle of Hastings.

Two surnames with virtually the same origins are **Freeborn** and **Freeman**. Robert Frebern who lived in Northumberland in 1163 inherited his name because his ancestors were either born free or inherited freedom. William Fremon who lived in Norfolk in 1196 obtained his freedom through some act for his lord and master and was rewarded with his freedom.

The Old English personal name *Ceadda* led to the surname **Chadd**. The Danish personal name *Algat* led to today's surnames **Allgood** and **Augood**. As with most Scandinavian names they were first more common in East Anglia. Robert Algood was a native of Suffolk in 1327. A popular first name was *Faeger*, Old English for the fair one. One early member of the family was Henry Fayrman, residing in Cornwall in 1297. Centuries later the surname is **Fairman**.

There are several origins of the surname **Beck**. Some members of the family originated from a village in Normandy named Bec. Others acquired it as they lived by a brook. It is thought that the majority acquired it from the Old English personal name *Beocca*, meaning pick-axe. Richard Becke was mentioned in Sussex records in 1296.

Probably one of the oldest Old English personal names, later used as a surname, was Dudd, mentioned in the Anglo-Saxon Chronicles with Aelfweard Dudd residing in Hampshire in 1030. It remains with us to this day as **Dodd**, **Dod** or **Dods**. **Dunstan** and **Dunstone** originated from Old English *Dunstan*, meaning hill stone. It was given to the man who lived near the stone on the hill, although some families may have acquired the name through residence in Dunstan, Northumberland. Margaret Dunstan resided in Kent in 1275. Another Old English personal name was *Lutta*, which led to the surname **Lutt**. One of the family ancestors was Simon Lutte who lived in Huntingdon in 1279.

The Saxons named him *Dreng*, but the Normans changed it to *Drenger*, meaning a young man. This name described a free tenant holding land, partly servile, partly military. A common name in Northumberland, we now know it as **Dreng** or **Dring**. Performing his part-time military service in Durham in 1155 was William Dreng.

One early Norman personal name was *Dolgfinnr* which became a common personal name in northern England just after the Conquest. It led to the modern surnames **Duffen** and **Dolphin**, with no connection with the sea creature of that name. Adam Dolfin was a resident of Durham in 1155.

Magnus, meaning great, was a Latin word which was passed down to early Norman. Magnus I was king of Norway and Denmark in 1047 and it was the name of many later Scandinavian kings; it also became very popular in the Shetlands. Today we know it as **Magnus** or **Manus**. By 1114 Hugo Magnus had found his way to Somerset. Another name with dual origins was old Norman *Sigarr* and Old Danish *Sighar*, meaning 'victory spear'. These led to the surname **Siggers** or **Siger**. Edricus Sigaros was mentioned in the Domesday Book of 1086 as holding land in Suffolk.

The Old Norman personal name *Hafleikr* meant seaport. How anyone came to acquire such a first name remains a mystery, but it led to the surname **Havelock**. We must presume that William Havelok who lived in Essex in 1327 resided near the coast. Another mystery, the Old Danish personal name *Orm* meant serpent. The surname **Orme** or **Orum** originated in Yorkshire but soon spread to other parts of the country. By 1275 one branch of the family, headed by John Orm, was living in Worcester.

A rare Scandinavian personal name that led to an unusual surname was *Tofa*. There is a record of Hildr, the daughter of Tofi. The name was found chiefly in Suffolk and occasionally in Essex and Norfolk. Two members of the family, both living in Norwich, were Stephen Tovild, 1473, and Alice Tovyld, 1491. Passed down through the generations, the surnames now are **Tovell**, **Tofield** and **Tufill**.

Another Swedish personal name was *Vigot*. One of the early holders was John Wiget, a resident of Worcester in 1180. Today the surnames are spelt **Wigget** and **Wicket**, the latter having nothing to do with the game of cricket. Not to be confused with **Capeman**, a man who made capes, the surname **Copeman** or **Coopman** originated from Old Norman *kaupmauer*, describing a merchant or travelling pedlar. It was also used as a personal name. Among the first of the family, John Copman was recorded in the Norfolk Pipe Rolls for 1205.

A surname that has remained unchanged since the Domesday Book is **Sprott** or **Sprot**. It stems from Old English *sprott*, meaning sprout or shoot, probably an agricultural term describing something or someone that was growing fast. There is record of a Sprot in the Essex division of the Domesday Book, and William Sprot lived in the same county in 1176.

A popular man in the village, always ready to give anyone a helping hand, soon earned the Old English name *Goldwine*, meaning good friend. This led to the surnames **Goldwin** and **Goldwyn**. One of the first was William Goldwyn, residing in Northumberland in 1256.

Among Old English personal names we find *Tunwulf*, *Tunric* and *Tunraed*. Saxon families often shortened these into pet names, usually *Tunna*. Later this became a surname in its own right, written as **Tunn**. One ancestor, Robertus filius Tunric, was recorded in the Bury St Edmunds Pipe Rolls for 1225.

There is nothing in the surname **Odd** to suggest the holder behaved any differently from the other villagers. It originated from the Old English personal name *Odda*. The Old Danish personal name *Ottar*, meaning 'terrible army', led to the respectable surname of **Otter**, which has nothing to do with the creatures that frequent river banks.

Another Old English personal name is *Beda*. It was in use centuries before the Norman Conquest. The most famous holder of this name was the Venerable Bede, who faithfully recorded Anglo-Saxon history up to the seventh century. Today we know the surname as **Bead** or **Beed**. If your surname is **Cade** or **Cadd**, have no fears that your ancestors were the village scoundrels. The name stems from Old English *Cada*, describing a stout or lumpish fellow. Thomas Kade lived in York in 1219, but William Cade resided miles away in Cornwall at the same time.

Irish surnames

Irish surnames originate from more sources than English or Scottish names yet, unlike their neighbours in England and Scotland, have fewer records or family papers to confirm them. This is understandable when one looks at Ireland's troubled history, punctuated by successive invasions, rebellions, agrarian disasters and mass emigration. Some Irish surnames are pure Gaelic or Irish, in use long before the English invasions, others were introduced by the Anglo-Normans, or by the Vikings; a few surnames are of dual origin, used by both the Irish and the English. Many Anglo-Normans who settled in Ireland took their names from Irish places. Centuries later, when the descendants of these settlers emigrated back to England, they took with them their surnames, by now regarded as pure Irish. Surnames prefixed with O' denote grandson while those prefixed with Mac denote son; these prefixes were added to the personal name of the grandfather or the father, irrespective of whether it was a personal or occupational name. Although it will be impossible to mention all the Irish surnames this chapter includes a broad selection with a note of the original dwelling places of some of the families where possible.

An early record lists Mugh Mac Cabe, who lived in 1386. The Irish spelling is Mac Caba, son of *Caba*, the cap or hood maker. The name today is **McCabe**. Always noted for its music and poetry, Ireland has special links for the families of **Reardon** or **O'Riordan.** It is taken from the Irish O'Rioghbhardain, descendant of *Rioghbhardan*, the royal bard. Maccret lived in Dublin in 1200. One of his descendants was Patric McRe who lived in Dublin in 1376. They were among the first of the **Macrae** and **McReath** families, who acquired their name from the Gaelic *Macrath*, son of grace.

Muircheartach Mac Taidhg lived in Ireland in 1159. A later member of the family was Mac Keg, who lived in 1511. They acquired their names from the Irish *Mac Taidhg*, son of Tadg, the poet, giving us the surnames **Keig** and **MacTague**. One of the dual origin surnames is **Lynch**. The Irish stems from O'loing Seachain, descendant of *Loingseach*, the sailor, resident in Thomond and Sligo, while the English Lynch was taken from the Old English word meaning dweller by the hill. The great **Murphy** clan of Leinster was centred in County Wexford. One of the early members was Domhnall-Dall-Ua-Murchadha who lived in 1127. The name was derived from *O'Murchadha*, grandson of the sea warrior.

Thomas de Joyce, a Welshman, emigrated to Ireland in 1283 and married the daughter of O'Brien, Prince of Thomond, and settled in County Galway. **Joyce** was derived from the birthplace of the Norman of that name of St Joss-sur-Mer in France. The first **Doyle** was O'Dubhghall who lived in AD 978 in south-east Leinster. He was a descendant of *Dubhghall*, the black stranger, probably a dark-skinned Dane.

The family of **Barrett** arrived with the Anglo-Norman invaders and settled in Galway and Munster. The name was taken from the Old French *barrette* and meant maker of caps. **Power** also arrived with the Anglo-Norman invasion, taken from the French *pohier*, meaning the man from Picardy.

Judging from the number of people named **Mulligan** and **Milligan**, several early Irishmen must have been bald as the name stems from *mael*, bald. Among the first families we find Molior Omolegane, Dublin, 1264. County Cork was, and still is, the birthplace of nearly all those born in Ireland with the name **O'Keefe**. One of the first was Art Caemh, son of the King of Munster, who lived in AD 902. The surname is probably derived from the Gaelic *cam*, meaning nose. The first **Fitzgerald** arrived with the Anglo-Normans. The entire family stems from Maurice, the son of Gerald, taken from an Old German word meaning 'spear ruler'. Two of the most influential Irish families, the Earls of Kildare and Dukes of Leinster, are Fitzgeralds. O'Coimin lived in Connaught in AD 600. He was the first of the **Cummíns**, whose name means descendant of the bent one. Possibly the greatest of all Irish surnames is **O'Brien**. Brian Boru was High King of Ireland, killed fighting at the Battle of Clontarf in 1014 when the Viking invaders were thrown back into the sea. All O'Briens, descendants of Brian, stem from this original family. On the other hand, **Burke** is an English name, derived from William de Burgo, from Burgh in Suffolk, who accompanied Henry II to Ireland in 1171. He settled in the country and later became Earl of Ulster. His surname gradually changed into Burke.

A very un-Irish-sounding name is **Bodkin**, a branch of the Fitzgerald family. They were descended from ancestors of the Earls of Desmond and Kildare. Richard Bodkin was an Irish landowner in 1242. They established themselves in the city of Galway around 1400; the name was probably derived from *bode*, meaning herald or messenger. **Boyle** has a fascinating history. Richard Boyle, an Englishman, landed in Ireland in 1588, later bought the properties of Sir Walter Raleigh and became Earl of Cork, his family becoming truly Irish. His son Robert Boyle was a famous mathematician and Fellow of the Royal Society. Boyle means 'the yellow haired one'. Another true Irish name is **Byrne**. The name was inherited from descendants of Bran. One member of the family was King of Leinster in 1052. The Normans drove them from their original home in County Kildare and they settled in south Wicklow. One of the most ancient Irish names is

81

MacCarthy. The name was derived from the son of Carthach, Lord of Edghannacht, descendant of the King of Munster. The surname originated from Caratacos, the ancient Briton taken to Rome as a prisoner. The family is thought to have emigrated from Wales to Ireland during the Roman occupation. The home of the family **McClancy**, son of *Flam*, the red one, was Counties Clare and Galway. Until the fourteenth century the family **Aherne** lived in lands near Six Mile Bridge, County Clare. They were Anglo-Norman immigrants who derived their name from Old English *hyrne*, resident in a nook or corner of land. **Athy** is very similar; living in Galway, they were immigrants from England and the name was derived from a word meaning dweller at the enclosure. William de Athy was Treasurer of Connaught in 1388. **MacCaffray** is derived from the Irish *Mac Gafraid*, son of Godfrey; Duncan MacGoffri lived in 1319.

No wonder the **Kelly** family have a reputation for fighting and feuding: the name is derived from O'Ceallaigh, descendant of *Ceallach*, the war lord. **O'Sullivan**, from the Irish O'Suileabhain, descendant of *Suileabhan*, the black-eyed one. More peaceful was **O'Clery**, from the Gaelic *O'Clerigh*, son of the clerk.

It is surprising how many Irish families were related to royal blood in medieval times, like **O'Flaherty** from *Flaithbheartaigh*, descendant of the bright ruler. James Ohagen lived in Dublin in 1280. His name was taken from the Irish O'Hagain, descendant of *Ogan*, the young one. The name has changed little; today we know it as **O'Hagan**. Another Dublin resident was Padyne Regane, 1264; his name came from *Riagin*, little king. The surname now is **O'Regan**. A name that rolls off the tongue is **O'Shea**, descendant of *Seaghda*, the stately or majestic one. A semi-royal family came from County Limerick: **O'Donovan** from the Gaelic *O'Donnabhain*, the brown one, possibly a Norseman of royal blood. Someone had to be around who could understand Gaelic, English, French and Scandinavian; the job fell to an **O'Driscoll**, from Gaelic *O'Heidersceoil*, the interpreter. The family of **Fitzpatrick** were of pure Gaelic descent, but at some time must have had some connection with the Romans. The surname was derived from *patraicc*, or patrician, meaning a Roman noble. The family was almost of royal blood: one was ruler of Leix. As a matter of interest, Patrick did not become popular as a Christian name in Ireland until the sixteenth century.

Those with the surname **Flynn** were renowned for their fiery nature. They are the descendants of O'Flainn, son of *Flann*, the one with the red hair. When did the first **O'Gallagher** sail across the seas to Ireland? O'Gallchobair, descendant of *Gallchobhar*, was himself descended from the King of Ireland, AD 654. The name means foreign help. The first **O'Hanly** was O'Hainle, the beautiful, and came from

Roscommon. The family of **O'Kelleher**, descendant of Kellener, nephew of the famous Brian Boru, lived in County Clare. Another nephew of Brian Boru was *Ceinneidgh*, known as ugly head. He lived at Glenmora near Killaloe; today we know the family as **Kennedy**. Laoghaire, the calf-keeper, lived in County Cork, which is still regarded by his descendants as home; we know them as **O'Leary**.

There were at least six tribes that contributed to the surname **O'Carroll**, mostly from Tipperary and Offaly. One early member of the family was O'Cearbhaill, meaning descendant of *Cearbhal*, who lived in 1014. Mahon was son of Murtagh Mor O'Brien, King of Ireland, who died in 1119; the family of **MacMahon** held lands in Corcabaskin, west Clare. A famous Ulster name is **O'Neill**, taken from the Irish *Niall*, meaning champion. The name was carried by Vikings from Ireland to Iceland, Norway and France, and eventually to England. **McAuliffe** originated in County Cork and was rarely found outside Munster. The name was derived from the Gaelic *Amlaib*, meaning 'a relic of the gods'. Richard Caddell, called Blake, was sheriff of Connacht in 1303 but **Blake** was not generally used as a surname until about 1700. It was used to describe someone dark in complexion. Another surname of Anglo-Norman origin is **Barry**. Philip de Barri held extensive lands in County Cork in 1179. The name originated from the French *barri*, dweller from the suburbs.

O'Daly means the honourable one. Cuconnacht O'Dalaigh lived in 1200; he was Baron of Magheradernon, County Westmeath. One of the descendants of Tadhg, King of Connacht, was O'Diarmaid, the free man. This family lived in Coolavin and are better known today as **MacDermot**. From Westmeath, an Anglo-Norman family was represented in 1185 by Godwin Dil, the grower or seller of the herb dill. The name has changed slightly and is now spelt **Dillion**. Domhnall lived in Kilmacrenan; his name originated from *domnall*, 'world mighty'. The family name is **O'Donnell**. Similar in spelling, but with an entirely different meaning, is **O'Donoghue**, descendant of *Donogh*, the brown warrior, from County Cavan. **McBrady** first resided near Cavan town, of Anglo-Norman extraction; the name derived from a maker of chords. **Breen** is one of the original Irish surnames; the family lived at Knocktopher, County Kilkenny. The name derives from a word meaning son of the noble, and the clan chief was Lord of Brawney in 1421. Mac Branain, chief of Corcachlan in 1159, was one of the early **Brennan** family; the name means descendant of the sad one. **McBride** and **McBryde** mean follower of St Bride, a family from Ulster, while **Cahill**, descendant of *Cathal*, meaning 'powerful in battle', lived in County Galway. Flann O'Cahill was martyred in AD 938. Members of the **O'Callaghan** family were descended from the King of Munster who lived in AD 952. The Gaelic name means son of the battle mighty.

Another name from an ancient Irish warrior is **McCann**. Amhlaibh Mac Canna, who lived in 1155, was the grandson of *Canna*, the war wielder. He was Lord of Clanbrassil and lived in County Armagh. **O'Casey** came from the Gaelic *caisin,* meaning the crooked one. The family were Lords of Swaithni Balrothery, County Dublin. More peaceful were the **O'Cassidy** family. They lived in Fermanagh and Giolla O'Cassidy, who lived in 1143, was a well-known Irish poet. The **O'Connor** family descended from Conchobhar (high will), King of Connacht in AD 971; the family also supplied two high kings of Ireland, one in 1086, the other in 1116. The Anglo-Norman **Collins** family came from Devon and settled in north Desmond. They became Lords of the Baronies of Connello. Collin was the pet name for Nicholas.

The Irish have long been famed for their literary skills and the name **Sheridan** ranks high in this field. The surname stems from the Irish O'Sirideain, descendant of *Siridean*, a personal name. The family originated in County Longford and the name is still found in great numbers in Cavan. Richard Brinsley Sheridan, the famous Dublin-born dramatist and theatre manager, dominated the London theatre scene in the late eighteenth century. The family of **Devine** can claim literary beginnings. It originated from the Irish O'Duibhin, descendant of *Duibhn*, the black poet. Nicholas le Devine had left his native shores and was resident in Hereford in 1187. From Dublin the surname of **Devlin** has spread world wide. The name means descendant of *Dobhailen*; William Develyn lived in London in 1380.

Kinsella is one of the few genuine native Gaelic surnames without the prefix Mac or O. The family descended from Dermot MacMurrough, ill-famed King of Leinster in the twelfth century. The surname was derived from Enna Cinnseallach and Domhnall Caomhanach, sons of that king. Today the family is found chiefly in the northern part of County Wexford. The Irish O'Cormaic, descendant of *Cormac* who was known as the son of the chariot, led to the surname **McCormack.** Little did Gillechrist Mac Cormac, living in Ireland in 1132, know that one of his descendants, John McCormack, the Irish-born tenor, would be known as the singer with the golden voice.

Both **Lammond** and **Lamont** stem from the Old Norman *Logmaor*, meaning law man. Laumannus filius Malcolmi resided in Ireland in 1230. Associated with the same surname is **MacLamon**, from the Gaelic *Maclaoumuinn*, descendant of Lamont. Both **Wolf** and **Woulfe** are from the Norman *woulf* (wolf) changed by the Irish to *De Bhulbh*. They settled in the County Kildare area and they had a home near Athy, known as Woulfe's Country. Captain George Woulfe of County Limerick was the great-great-grandfather of General Wolfe, who captured Quebec in 1759. Both **Kehue** and **Keogh** were Norman families who hailed from Caieu, France. They settled in the parish of Taghmaconnel; the place Keoghuille is named after them. Maolmuire Mackeogh was an Irish poet living in Leinster in 1534. **Lally** is a shortened version of O'Mullally; they originally settled in Tuam. **O'Hurley**, from the Anglo-Norman *Hurley*, was changed to the Irish Urley, son of Blod, son of Cas, founder of the Irish family. They first settled in northern Tipperary. O'Hurley was one of the principle chiefs of Thomond in 1309.

Many Irish names feature in haunting songs, and **O'Dooley** is one of them. They are the descendants of *Donndubhan*, the dark one. The O'Dubhlaich were Lords of Fertullagh in the eleventh and twelfth centuries. They first settled in County Westmeath and now live mainly in Leix and Offaly. **O'Farrell**, with or without the prefix O', is one of the most common Irish surnames. It may have originated from the Old French *ferour* denoting a smith or worker in iron. Originally they resided in County Longford and the chief resided at Longphuirt at O'Farrell's Fortress.

O'Boyle is from the Gaelic word for pledge. The chief was seated at Cloghineely. Ballyweel, near Donegal town, was known as the home of the O'Boyles. At one time they were noted for their ruddy complexion. The **O'Cooney** family originated in County Tyrone. It is thought the name stemmed from the old English *cony*, meaning rabbit. They migrated southwards to north Connacht and Diarmio O'Cuana resided a few miles away in Elphin in 1248. **Mulcahy** comes from the Irish *O'Maolchathaigh*, meaning warlike. The clan originated in south Tipperary but later moved to south Munster. **MacQuilly** is the Gaelic form of Cox. The name stems from the Gaelic *Mac An Choiligh*, descendant of the cock. The surname is still common in County Roscommon, the place of its birth. **Cusack** is a Norman name introduced into Ireland after the invasion of 1172. The surname was derived from a French place, Guienne, then anglicised as De Cussac. Geoffrey and André de Cusack landed in Ireland with King John in 1211 and obtained lands in Meath. **Dalton**, again not Irish in its origins, was first recorded in Ireland following King John's invasion. Legend has it that the first Dalton fled to England after secretly marrying the daughter of the King of France. After arriving in England they settled in Dalton, Durham, before joining King John's campaign. The family acquired lands in Teffia, Meath, and some descendants still live in Westmeath. Another Anglo-Norman family to settle in Ireland after the invasion was the **Costello** family. The family was originally called Nangles. In 1193 they occupied parts of Connacht. The family named their sons *Distealb*, son of Gilbert de Nangle, then called *Mac Oisoealbhaigh*, anglicised to Mac Costello. **MacCoy** is chiefly found in and around Ulster. The family first came from the Scottish Western

Isles. It became the Irish *Mac Aodha* (descendant of Hugh).

O'Beirne started out as *Biorn*, the raven. The family was exclusive to Connacht, one branch displacing the O'Monahans. They occupied the area between Elphin and Boyle. From the same family and surname source we get the surnames **Byrne** and **Birn**, descendants of Bran, a relation of Biorn. **MacGeraghty** and **Jerety** originate from the Irish O'Roduibh. The family was wide spread in Roscommon and Galway. MacGiriaaht was chief of the clan in Athlone in 1585. From the Gaelic *vidhir*, meaning dun-coloured, came the family name of **Maguire**. They lived mainly in County Fermanagh in the early days. Nicholas Maguire resided in Enniskillen in 1460 and there is record of a Maguire, Baron of Enniskillen, in the 1650s. The O'Mulryan clan became the **Ryan** family, originally located in the Limerick–Tipperary borders. One member of the family was Eamonn O'Ryan, 1680.

There were two branches of the **Sarsfield** family who occupied lands in Dublin, County Cork and County Limerick. The name originated from Sarsfield in Kent, now lost. Thomas de Sarsfield was chief standard bearer to Henry II in 1172. William de Sharisford settled in Ireland in 1252 and the family were granted lands in 1300. One branch of the family later became the Earls of Lucan. The Gaelic *O'Siddhachan*, meaning peaceful, became the surname **Sheahan**, from Cork, Kerry and Limerick. They were hereditary trumpeters to the chiefs of the great clans. O'Sheaghyn, 1543, was trumpeter to the great O'Kelly. There are two branches of the **Tracy** family, one English, one Irish. The name originated from Traci in France, and the Irish branch became O'Treasaigh. O'Tressy of Cloncurry was recorded as living in the locality in 1304.

O'Quigley and **Cogley** stem from the Irish O'Coigligh, descendant of *Coigleach*, the untidy one. Now usually written without the prefix O', the family first lived in County Mayo. Now the name is commonplace in the Derry, Donegal and Sligo areas. From the son of *Conn*, meaning counsel, we get the surnames **Quinn** and **O'Quinn**. Today it can be found in all parts of Ireland, but it first appeared in Tyrone. We have an early record of Niall O'Cuinn residing near Omagh in 1014. In the early eighteenth century many emigrated to France, and even today there is a rue O'Quinn in Bordeaux.

The **O'Toole** family are today mostly concentrated in Dublin City and County. The name stems from *O'Tuathail*, mighty people. Some members of the family have acquired the surname **Toal**. Laurence O'Toole was Archbishop of Dublin in 1171. Some members of the family fought in the Irish Brigade of the French Army in the eighteenth century and are ancestors of the present Count O'Toole of Limoges.

Members of the **Molloy** family have a distinguished origin. The name stems from the Irish word for noble or venerable chieftain . They are descended from Niall, King of Ireland in AD 371. Albin O'Molloy resided at Tullamore in 1223. **Redmond** in Irish is Reamonn (Raymond), son of Bemund. The family came over with William the Conqueror and settled in Ireland after the Norman invasion. The name meant 'might protection'. The first of the Irish family was Alexander Raymond; in the next generation the name became Redmond. They were granted extensive lands in County Wexford.

Another Anglo-Norman family that established themselves soon after the Norman invasion of Ireland was the **Moore** or **O'More** family. The original Irish family were known as *O'Mordha*, stately noble, and they have St Fintan as their protector. This is the family name of the Earls of Drogheda. Rory O'More resided in Dublin in 1557.

Although **Ward** is a common English surname the majority of Irish Wards are native Irish in their origins. The Gaelic name stems from *Mac An Bhaird*, descendant of the bard, and the early members of the family were professional bards. In the early days they were found mostly in Donegal and Galway.

What better name to finish with than **Malone**. It stems from the Irish *O'Maoileoin*, the servant of St John. The name is celebrated in the famous song in which sweet Molly Malone wheels her barrow 'through streets wide and narrow, crying "Cockles and mussels, alive, alive–o!". Although now wide spread, the name first appeared in the Dublin area.

Scottish surnames

Scottish surnames are not as old as their English counterparts. The first surnames used in Scotland were of Norman origin. Later it became usual for a laird to take his name from the estate, which in turn had been named from the owner. The clan system afforded men the chance to attach themselves to a powerful group, a means of insurance in troubled times. But when surnames did begin to be used, generally in the sixteenth century, they followed the pattern of English surnames and were given as nicknames, occupational surnames or place names. After 1820, the steady influx of the Irish into south-west Scotland caused widespread corruption of surnames. A Gaelic surname does not prove Scottish descent, and some people with pure English surnames are of Scottish descent.

Many Scottish surnames were derived from the original homes of the first holders; some even have the triple distinction of being first names, surnames and place names. **Brodie** and **Brady** were first recorded in 1311 with Michael de Brothie of Brody, Morayshire. From Buchan in Aberdeenshire comes **Buchan**; an early holder of the name was Richard de Buchan in 1207. Robert de Leslie, 1272, was one of the first of the Leslie family which inherited its name from **Leslie** in Fife. Malcolm de Drumond, the first of the **Drummond** family, acquired his name in 1270 from the Barony of Drummond. Ayrshire gave us the **Cunningham** family, first recorded in 1210 with Richard de Cunningham, from Cunningham. Duncan de Forbeys, the first of the **Forbes,** acquired his name in 1272 from Forbes, Aberdeenshire. **Gordon** owes its name to Ricker de Gordun; he took it from the Barony of Gordon in the Scottish Borders in 1150. Archibald de Levingestoune, who lived in Livingston, West Lothian, in 1296, gave us the surname **Livingston**. William de Moravia lived in the province of Moray; from him descended the family surname **Murray**. The Old Irish *dubh-glass* meant black water. This nickname was given to William de Duglas in 1175, leading to the surname **Douglas**, also the name of Douglas, Lanarkshire. **Dougal** came from similar origins – Old Irish *dubhgall*, meaning black stranger; a later surname, it was first recorded in 1152 but not used very much until the sixteenth century. **Ramsay** and **Ramsey** both owe their origins to a Simund de Ramesie who, in 1175, left his native Ramsey, Huntingdon, in England and settled in Scotland. **Cameron** was derived from two sources, from the Gaelic *camshron*, meaning hook nose (the highland clan), and from Cameron, Fife (the Lowland name). Adam de Kamerum who lived in 1214 was from the Lowlands.

Are you a **Campbell**? Your name originated from the Gaelic *caimbeal*, meaning crooked mouth. Records fail to reveal why Colin Campbell was given this nickname in 1282. On the other hand, the name of **Duncan** stems from the Gaelic *donn chadh*, meaning brown warrior, given to John Duncan of Berwick in 1367. The Gaelic *fearchar* was an endearing term meaning 'very dear one', leading to the surnames **Farquhar** and **Farquharson**; Andro Farchare lived in 1450. **Ferguson** is easy, son of Fergus, which was Old Irish for 'man choice'; no one knows why John Fergusson received this nickname in 1466. **Gow** should be as common as Smith; it is derived from the Gaelic *gobha*, meaning smith. There are not many early records; the first one appears in 1380 with George Gow.

Now we come to the Macs, which of course mean 'son of'. One could fill a book with these, but here are a few; some speak for themselves, others have more quaint origins. **Macpherson** was son of the parson; an early holder of the name was Alexander Makfersan, 1447. Another name that is common is **MacTavish**, derived from son of Tammas, Lowland Scots for Thomas; it is recorded in 1355 with Duncan Mc Thamais. **Malcolmson** needs no explaining; Symon Malcomesson took his father's name of Malcolm in 1296. Both **Macrae** and **McRea** stem from an old personal name meaning 'son of grace'; no reason is given why Alexander Macrad was given the name in 1225. Malcolm McIvyr was given his name in 1292. It meant the son of Ivor, which in turn meant 'bow army'; now we know it as **MacIver**. Matthew McNab who lived in 1376 was the son of Nab, a Gaelic name for an abbot, and the first of all today's families named **MacNab**.

Ronald Makalestyr, 1455, was the son of Alexander, and the family lives on as **McAllister**. Dungall McAlayne, son of Allain, lived in 1376; he passed on the family surname **MacAllan**. Probably the most famous of all Scottish names, **MacBeth** was an Old Gaelic personal name meaning 'son of life'. Cristinus McBryd, 1329, received his nickname from son or servant of St Bride. It has been passed down as **McBride**. An unusual one, **McCall**, first recorded in 1370 with Robert McKawele, signified a son of Kathal. **McConachie** was derived from son of Duncan, while **Macfarlane** stems from son of Farlan. Maurice McGill was the son of the stranger; the surname is still known as **McGill**. One of the proudest names must be **Mackintosh** or **McIntosh**; one of the first holders was Farchard McToschy in 1382. It means son of the chieftain.

A place name in Aberdeenshire is the origin of at least seven surnames, including **Crombie**, **Crumbie** and **Crummy**. Among the early holders of this surname we find Patrick of Cromby, 1423, Robert Crumby, 1450, and David Crommy, 1516.

The Scottish pronunciation of Peter or Patrick resulted in the surnames **Petrie**, **Peatrie** and **Patry**. Charles Patre resided at Dunkeld in

1513. There are at least eight variations of the surname **Moffat** or **Muffat**, first given to a man who lived at or hailed from Moffat, Dumfries. We have records of two early residents of the town, Nicholas de Mufet, 1232, and Thomas Moffett, 1296. Crawford, a small Lanarkshire village on the site of an old Roman road, led to the surname **Crawford**. John de Crauford, a local resident in 1147, left his mark in local records. Many miles away, the village of Strachan, Aberdeenshire, gave birth to the surname **Strachan** or **Strahan**.

Craig is the Scottish version of *cragg*, meaning 'dweller by the steep rugged rocks'. It was probably a spartan existence for John de Crag, living in the wilderness in 1143. A similar surname, **Craigie** was taken from the place name of Craigie in Aberdeenshire, Ayrshire and Perthshire. A few members of the family may have acquired the surname through residence at Craggan, a tiny hamlet near Grantown-on-Spey, or its namesake, a cluster of cottages facing Loch Long, Dunbartonshire. Brice de Cragy, 1317, was one of the first to bear the name.

One Old English female pet name that found its way to Scotland was *Goldie*, meaning 'the one with fair hair'. It found its way north of the border at the end of the sixteenth century. By some quirk of fate it became popular in Edinburgh, where we find records of a John Gowdie in 1602. Eventually the surname became **Goudie** or **Goudy**. One would be hard put to think of a more Scottish name than **Haggis** but it has nothing to do with the culinary delight of the nation. It stems from hag-house, a woodcutter's hut, at one time a common place name. Some families may have originated from Haggbeck, Roxburgh, in the Scottish Borders. Gilbert of Haggehouse, 1394, probably lived near a woodcutter's cottage.

The city of Edinburgh produced several surnames, including **Edinborough**, **Edinbry** and **Edynbry**. Among its medieval citizens we find Alex Edenburg, 1240, Alexander de Edynburgh, 1223, and Thomas Edynburgh, 1396.

Old French *debonnaire* was shortened to *bonnaire*, meaning gentle or courteous. Although the nickname was used on both sides of the border, it became very popular in Scotland, resulting in the surname **Bonner**. William Boner was an Aberdeen resident in 1281 and William Bonour a citizen of St Andrews in 1451.

Citizens of the Midlothian town of Currie took the surname **Currie** world wide. Phillip de Curry lived in the locality in 1179. **McAdam**, a name made famous by the road builder, meant the son of Adam.

Gaelic *Macascaidh*, meaning son of Ascaidh, was taken from the pet name of Askell. Gilbert Makasky emigrated from Scotland to the Isle of Man in 1318. Today, the family name is **MacKaskie** or **MacAskill**.

There are several sources for the surname **Mailer**. The Scottish version stems from the lost place Mailer, Forteviot, near Perth. John de Malere lived in Perth in 1296. A similar surname, **Mair**, came from the Gaelic *maor* and Scottish *mair*, describing an officer of the law who executed legal writs and also deputised as a king's herald or in other official posts. It is doubtful if Symon de Mare who lived around Perth at the end of the thirteenth century was popular with the local folk as he distributed his master's royal commands to all and sundry.

From Eskdale, Dumfries, came the families of **Esdaile**, **Esdale** and **Isdale**. Among their ancestors were John de Esdale, 1413, and Margaret Eskdale, 1472. Balhousie in Fife was the birthplace of the **Boosie**, **Bousie** and **Bowsie** families. There are few early records of the name, but we do know of a John Bousie, resident in the area in 1566.

Kirkland was the birthplace of the families with that surname; there are two of them, both in Dumfries. One is a tiny hamlet, north of Dumfries, the other a small group of houses just outside Sanquhar. John de Kyrkeland resided on the edge of Dumfries in 1280.

From a lost village in the Scottish Borders comes the surname **Dalgleish**. It is possible the name also stemmed from the small hamlet of Dalguise, adjacent to the Craigvinean Forest in Perth. Only one early record of the name exists, Symon de Dalgles, 1407.

The English had a pet name for Adam – Atkin. When the name was introduced across the border, the Scottish translated it to Aiken. This in turn led to the surnames **Aitken** and **Aiken**. Andrew Atkin who lived in 1405 probably took his father's first name as his own surname.

The village of Dunning, straddling crossroads in Lower Strathearn, Perth, gave rise to the surname **Dunning**. From people like Gillemichael de Dunin, 1208, and John Dunning, 1321, the surname has now spread over the entire English-speaking world.

An uncomplimentary nickname that later became a surname was **Cruikshanks**, derived from the Old Norman *krokr*, meaning hook, and Old English *sceana*, meaning shank, resulting in 'crooked leg'. No doubt John Crokeshanks who hobbled about in Haddington in 1296 was stung by his fellow villagers' cruel remarks.

Bruce must be one of the proudest Scottish surnames. The original member of the family was a Norman from Brix, northern France. Adam de Brus was awarded lands after the Norman invasion. His son became a friend of David I, King of Scotland, and was granted the Lordship of Annandale in 1124. His second son, Robert, became the founder of the Scottish house of Bruce. Eventually the clan owned lands in Annandale, Clackmannan and Elgin. It is likely that many followers or workers on the estates embraced the surname.

Common in Angus, the surname **Eason** or **Esson** was derived from the Scottish form of 'son of Adam'. The surname **Angus** was derived from the Gaelic *Aonghus*, meaning unique or from residence in Angus.

Soon after the Battle of Hastings the family of **Manners** settled in southern England, taking their name from their birthplace, Mesnières in Normandy. A while later branches of the family moved to Scotland, where the name became **Menzies**. The first record of the family in Scotland was noted in 1306 with one De Meinzels.

At least twenty-three variations of the surname **Neil** or **Neal** are known. The name originated from the Gaelic *Niall*, meaning champion. The Scandinavians took it from Scotland to Iceland, then on to Norway. From here the name was taken to France, and eventually England. The first Scottish families included Achyne Mac Nele, 1289, and Neil Carrick from Galloway in 1314.

The surnames **Anderson** and **MacAndrew** are closely linked by similar origins. Both mean the son of Andrew. One famous ancestor, John MacAindrea, was known as Little John, a man widely feared by cattle rustlers of Lochaber owing to his prowess as a bowman. Another member of the family was Henry Androsoun who lived in the locality in 1443.

Famous for the invention of television, the surname **Baird** was taken from a Greek nickname meaning 'to dress richly', a title that was probably rare in medieval Scotland. Thomas Baird owned lands in Auchmeddan as early as 1297.

Here are three surnames with true Gaelic origins. **MacKay** is taken from the Gaelic *Mac Addha*, meaning son of Aodh (for example Gilnen McCay, 1506). **MacLean** comes from Gaelic *Mac Gilleenin*, son of the servant of St John (Alexander McKleane, 1684). **McTurk** is from the Gaelic *Mac Tuirc*, son of Torc (John Makturk, 1538).

Richard de Boulden lived in the small village of Bowden, just outside Melrose. The family today is still known as **Bowden**. There is very little doubt concerning the origins of **Glasgow**. John de Glasgu lived in the city in 1258. **Glendenning** arose in Glendinning Westerkirk in Dumfries, whilst **Arras** stems from the lost place Airhouse, Channelkirk, in the Scottish Borders.

Situated on the road between Greenlaw and Berwick-upon-Tweed, a small group of cottages gave its name to the surname **Blackadder**. Adam of Blacathathir resided in Berwick in 1426. **Blackwood** stemmed from a place of that name in Lanarkshire; Robert Blakwode dwelt in the district in 1384.

Scott is one of the most numerous Scottish surnames. It derives from Old English *Scott*, meaning a Gael from Scotland and was particularly common in the border region. A considerable number of Scottish soldiers who obtained employment as retainers in England assumed the surname as a matter of course. When David I, King of Scotland, acquired the lands of the Earl of Huntingdon through marriage, he sent soldiers and other Scottish retainers to work and guard them. This is one reason why so many men with the surname Scott were found in East Anglia in the early fourteenth century.

Geoffrey de Mallaville took his name from his birthplace, Emalleville in Normandy. He settled in Midlothian, naming the place Melville, and thus creating the surnames **Melvill** and **Melvin**. One of the first in the region was Hugh de Malleville, 1202. Both **MacLeod** and **McCloud** are derived from the Old Norman *ljiotr*, meaning 'son of Leod'. John McCloud, an Edinburgh resident, qualified as a doctor in 1621.

The first name of Patrick led to the surnames **Patterson** and **Paterson**. Two branches of the family from Aberdeen were those of William Patrison, 1446, and Donald Pattryson, 1490. From the same source we get **Pattison** and **Patison**, both derived from Paton, an alternative name for Patrick. Gavin was a popular Scottish first name which led to the surnames **Gawenson** and **Ganson**, meaning son of Gavin.

From the Scottish *mekil*, meaning big, sprang the surnames **Meikle** and **Mickle**. No doubt William Mykyl, 1382, walked head and shoulders above his fellow villagers. This in turn led to **Meklejohn** and **Mucklejohn**, indicating 'big John'. Perhaps William Meiklejohne, 1638, was not one to argue with.

Berowald of Flanders arrived with William the Conqueror. In the twelfth century, seeking pastures new, one branch of the family moved to Scotland, where Malcolm IV granted them a charter of lands in Moray. They took this place as their surname, which to this day remains as **Innes**.

Holders of the surnames **Dunce**, **Duns** or **Dunse** need not fear their ancestors were stupid. The surnames were derived from residence in the town of Duns, formerly the county town of Berwickshire but now in the Scottish Borders. Hugh de Duns, 1150, must have been a man of some position and learning to have his name recorded in local documents.

Durward is one of the few original Scottish occupational surnames. It began with the office of 'door-ward', a hereditary position that was passed down from father to son. Alan Durward, Justiciar of Scotland, who died in 1268, was the son of Thomas Dorward. The surname was more common in the Arbroath area, no doubt because there would have been door-wards in the twelfth-century abbey. From a lost place in Dumfries, Culewen, came the surname **Curwen**. Gilbert de Culewen resided in the locality in 1262. A similar name, **Cullen**, was given to one who lived or came from the town of that name in Moray. Residing in the town in 1340 was Henry de Culane.

The family of **Gunn** are of Norse descent. The name stems from *gunnr*, meaning battle. Once established in Scotland, the family obtained lands in Caithness and Sutherland. George Gunn, a clan leader, was slain during a clan war in the fifteenth century.

Both Scottish **Home** and **Hume** originated when the family were given the Barony of Home. Over the years the family acquired lands in the border country. William of Home, 1268, cannot have known that one of his descendants would one day be British Prime Minister.

McKenna was derived from the Gaelic *Maccionaodha*, the son of Cionaodm. **McAlpine** stems from son of Alpin. John MacAlpyne was mentioned in Scottish records in 1260.

Records show that the first **Graham** to settle in Scotland was William de Graham, 1127, a Norman who brought with him the Norman version of his surname, which was derived from the town of Grantham, where the family had first settled. But legend has it that a Graham lived in Scotland centuries before this during the Roman occupation of Britain. He breached the Antonine Wall, a defensive barrier erected by the Romans to stop the Scots attacking Roman-held territory. This place became known as Graeme's Dyke. Whether this was true or not, the Grahams flourished, acquiring lands in the Trossachs and around Kincardine Castle.

Old English *stigweard*, meaning 'a keeper of the house', led to the surnames **Stewart**, **Steward** and **Stuart**. From keeper of the house, the steward became the official who controlled the domestic affairs of a large household and progressed further to officer of the royal household, steward of a manor, or manager of a large estate. The Lord High Steward of Scotland was the first royal officer, second only to the monarch. Among early members of the family we have Phelippe Styward of Roxburgh, 1296. Robert the Steward became the Scottish King Robert II and founded the royal house of Stuart.

Finlay or **Finlow** can be spelt at least six different ways. The name stems from the Gaelic *fionnlagh*, meaning 'fair hero'. Andrew Fyndelai, 1526, had a son who was named John Finlason, the son of Finlay, which led to the surnames **Finlayson** and **Finlason**. Another name with a similar origin is **Bain**, taken from the Gaelic *ban*, meaning fair or white. Thomas Ban was a citizen of Perth in 1324.

Fraser originated from the Norman *friselle*, strawberry flowers. After branches of the family emigrated to Scotland they acquired lands in East Lothian. Sir Alexander Fraser founded the port of Fraserburgh in the late sixteenth century. Both **Cochrane** and **Colqueran** were taken from the family birthplace, Cochrane in Renfrewshire.

Both **Coltard** and **Coltart** are agricultural occupational surnames. Old English *colt-hierde* described the keeper of the colts, and the surname found its way to Scotland. By 1627 John Coltart was residing in Dumfries. The Old English first name *Elwald* became the surname **Elliot**. Later families may have acquired the name through residence at Eliot in Angus.

MacEwen originated from the Gaelic *Maceoghainn*, son of Eden. There was a Gilpatrik MacEwen in 1219. **McFadden** came from the Gaelic *Macpaaidon*, son of Paiden or 'Little Pat'. Donald M'Fadzeane is mentioned in 1473. **MacFarlon** originated from the Gaelic *MacPharlain*, son of Parlan. Malcolm McPharlane was recorded in 1385.

Today the surname **Burns** is treated with reverence throughout the world by Scotsmen. Robert Burns's ancestors lived in Burnhouse in North Ayrshire, from where they obtained their name. This place name may have had some connection with the cruel medieval punishment of burning people's hands. One early member of the family was David Burnis, resident in Ayrshire in 1526.

Welsh surnames

Hereditary surnames were not generally used in Wales until about 1600 and even then some families refused to use them. Many of our modern surnames derive from Old Welsh personal names that started in England long before they were used in Wales. About the time of Henry VIII, the Welsh gentry began to adopt surnames, but the custom spread more slowly among the common folk.

In the same way as Mac means 'son of' in Ireland and Scotland, Ap means 'son of' in Welsh names. Edeneut Ap Ievan, the son of Evan, lived close to the English border in 1287, and a little later in 1300 we find a Howell ap Evan living close by. *Ap Evan*, the son of Evan, was responsible for the surnames **Bevan, Beven** and **Beavon. Harvard** was introduced by the Bretons. It meant 'battle worthy', from the French *hervé*. Not only was it eventually adopted by the Welsh, it was among the first of the surnames used in the American colonies and is today the name of America's most famous college.

A popular forename after the Norman Conquest was the Teutonic *Hugo*, and one of the first Welsh records quotes Richard Ap Hughe who lived in north Wales in 1563. From this one forename has sprung about twenty surnames, with another ninety variations; the Welsh ones include **Hughes, Huws, Hewes, Howes** and **Pugh**. It was introduced into Wales from north-west England and Ireland. **Humphries** stemmed from the German *hunfrid,* protector of the house, and **Hunt** from the Old English *hunta*, a huntsman. **James** started out as the Hebrew Jacob and then became Jacomus; from this stemmed the French Jacques, English Jacob and Welsh Iago. Old English *cniht* led to today's **Knight**. At first it referred to a servant, then a feudal tenant bound to serve as a mounted soldier; at times it just described a common soldier. Mereduht Ap Grifin, now **Meredith**, originated from the Welsh *morgetiud.* **Morris** came from the Latin *mauritius*, meaning swarthy or dark-skinned (the Welsh were considerably darker than their fair-skinned Anglo-Saxon neighbours).

Philip Ap Howel lived in Powys in 1285; we next hear of the name in Flintshire with Richard Ap Hoell in 1544. These were the forerunners of today's **Powell**, the son of Howel. **Price** originated from the son of Rhys; the first record of the name came from London with Jorwerth Ap Reys in 1393. John Aprice lived in Pembroke in 1492. The forename of Rhys provided another surname – **Rees** or **Rhys**. The Old Welsh for this name was *Ris*, 'the fervent one'. Griffinus filius Res lived adjacent to the Shropshire border in 1198.

Again from Shropshire into Wales we find **Saunders**, a pet form of Sander, derived from Alexander; a man named Sander lived in

Shropshire in 1255. From the Welsh *fychan,* meaning small or little, stemmed **Vaughan**; this surname was used in Wales as early as 1222 with Grifit Vehan of Brecon. Both **Walshman** and **Welshman** were given to men from Wales who settled elsewhere; one such man was John Walshman, a tailor who lived in London in 1324.

The French called him Guillaume, the Normans Willelm, and the English William. After the Conquest this became the most popular Christian name until superseded by John. It became common in Wales, and today the surname **Williams** is just as popular. **Watkins** derives from Wat-kin, a pet form of Walter; Watkynge Llooyde who lived in 1623 adopted it as his surname. **Bedward** and **Beddard** both derive from Ap-Edward, the son of Edward; one of the first holders of the surname was Dafydd Ap Edward who resided in Wales in 1498. **Beynon** stemmed from Ap Einon; we find the earliest record of the surname in Powys with Cadugan Ap Eynon who lived in 1285. Madocus Ap Oweyn was one of the first of the family **Bowen**; he lived in Wales in 1292.

For centuries the people of Wales have had much in common with the residents of Cornwall. Both areas were the last strongholds of the Britons, so it is only natural that one should come across the surname **Britton**. In the first place the name originated in Cornwall and was used to describe a man from Brittany. For example, John de Bretayne who lived in Cornwall in 1327 could claim that his ancestors did originate in Brittany. Later the name was used in the Welsh border counties to describe a true Welshman.

In medieval times few people possessed full municipal rights; the French called such a man a *bureis.* This led to the surname **Burgess** which later applied to the inhabitant of a borough or a freeman of such a borough. **Daniels** was first used in the eastern counties, then found its way to the border counties, and from there into Wales. It was a Hebrew name meaning 'God has judged'. **Davey** and **Davies** are from David, which in Welsh means 'friend', and the name has been in common use in Wales for more than nine centuries. **Edwards** stemmed from the Old English *eadweard*, prosperity guard; one of the early holders of the name was John Edwards, a Welshman who lived in 1498.

Evans, son of Evan, the Welsh form of John, dates from about 1500. It was used in England before this date, chiefly in Suffolk. The surnames **Ennion** and **Eynon** derive from the Welsh *einon*, meaning anvil, a nickname for one with fortitude and stability. Eynon Eynun lived on the border near Shropshire in 1221. **Francis** originally referred to a Frank (German), then later to a Frenchman, and was then used by Englishmen living in the border counties to describe a Welshman. Henry, and the son of Henry, resulted in the surnames **Harries**,

Harris and **Harry**; William Harrys was a Welshman living in 1406.

Griffin commenced with the Domesday Book; it was introduced into the eastern counties by the Bretons and at about the same time appeared in the border counties with the Welsh. It stemmed from the pet form of the Old Welsh *Gruffudd* and one early holder of the name was Griffin filius Gurgan who lived in Pembroke in 1130. Another well-established name was **Griffiths** from the Old Welsh *Griph-Ivo*, later Grufudd, meaning 'Griffin-the-Chief'. The name was first noted in Wales in 1150.

Among the oldest of true Welsh names we find **Howells**, from Old Welsh *Houel* and Breton *Huwel*. Huwal was king of West Wales in AD 926 and Morganus filius Hoel (who was born an Englishman) lived in Shropshire in 1166. Welsh people have always been renowned for the tone of their voices and the strength of their vocal cords, especially if their name is **Lewis**. The name is the Anglo-French form of the Teutonic *hludwig,* meaning 'loudest in battle'; the Welsh used the name as a shortened version of Llewelyn. In 1413 Llewelyn Ap Madoc became known as Lewis Madoc. **Llewelyn** is often said to mean fearless as a lion but probably stems from *llyw*, meaning leader. **Lloyd** stems from the Welsh *llwyd* meaning grey; one exile from the valleys of Wales was Richard Loyt who in 1327 was living in Worcester.

Morgan has a variety of origins. The Breton, Cornish and Welsh version was *Morcant*, while the Picts had *Morgunn*. It is one of the oldest Celtic names and means a sea dweller. **Owens** came from the Old Welsh *eugein,* taken from a Greek word meaning well born. The name was also introduced into England by the Bretons. **Ewens** has the same source. As early as 1086, Ewen the Breton was living near the Herefordshire border, and in 1200 Robertus Filius Ywein is recorded in the same area.

The surname **Jennifer** stems from the Welsh *Gwenhwyvar*, a female first name from *gwen*, meaning fair or white, and *gwyf*, smooth or fair. It became *Gwenhevare* across the border in Shropshire by the early fifteenth century. A few years later the name was written as Jenefer and had become Juniper in the seventeenth century. There seems to be some connection between the original Welsh forename and that of the legendary King Arthur's queen Gwenivere. **Wales** or **Wailes** was the name given by English folk to those of Welsh origin who had settled in England. It was taken from Old English *walh* denoting a foreigner. William le Wales resided in Lincoln in 1275, a long way from his native Wales. There is a locality not far from Sheffield that was named Wales in 1291, suggesting that a number of Welsh migrants were living in the vicinity. Another name given to the Welsh was the Anglo-French *Waleis* or *Walais*, meaning the Welshman or Celt. It became the surname **Wallis** and was taken as a surname by many English families living near the Welsh border. Richard le Walles lived in Shrewsbury in 1225.

Both **Penry** and **Pendry** originate from the Welsh Ap Henry. Again, members of the family moving into England in medieval times took their name with them. One was Howel Ap Henri, mentioned in parliamentary records in 1316. Joan Pendrie lived in Hereford in 1605.

A few Welsh names originated from Latin, among them **Cecil** and **Saycell**. These began with the Welsh *Seisill*, from the Latin *Caecilius*. Among the early holders of the name were William Selsil who lived near the Hereford border in 1205. From Latin *Caius* came the Welsh *Kei*, also used by Bretons and Cornish folk. This later became the surname **Keyse**, used by people on both sides of the Welsh border. Cecilla De Kays resided in Hereford in 1289.

Another surname derived from a first name, **Uprichard** came from Ap Richard. Robert Upprichard was living in Cheshire in 1637. The surname **Gwyn** is Welsh for white. Thomas Gwyn was a doctor in Oxford in 1528, and there was the famous Nell Gwynn who captivated Charles II. **Cadogan** stemmed from the Old Welsh *Cadwugaun*; Cadegan de Middleton lived a stone's throw from Shrewsbury in 1191. **Gronow** originated from the Welsh *Goronwy* or *Gronin*. Kenring Ap Grono resided near Chirk in 1391. From the Celtic *cynwrig*, meaning chief-man, evolved the surname **Kenrick**. Hugo filius Chenwrec lived near Llangollen in 1166 while Richard Kendrick and his family had moved to Chester by 1593.

Jevons originated from the Welsh *Ievan*, later spelt *Even*, the Welsh version of John. Jevan Thomas resided in Glamorgan in 1600. The three surnames **Pumfrey**, **Ponfrey** and **Boumphrey** are closely connected; all stem from Ap Humphrey. Edward Ap Humphrey moved from Wales to Shrewsbury in 1575, while Anable Pumfrey resided on the Welsh side of the border in 1633. Very few Welsh surnames originate from a place of birth but one exception is **Gower** or **Guwer**. These families first came from the Gower peninsular. Walter de Guher had moved from his birthplace to Carmarthen by 1130. There are many Welsh place names that begin with the prefix *Pont*, Anglo-French for bridge. The surname **Ponter** described the dweller by or keeper of the bridge, and the surname found its way over the border into Wales. Richard Ponter resided near Pontfadoc.

One of the most popular forenames introduced by the Normans into England was Richard. At least twenty different surnames evolved from this forename. It soon became popular in Wales, where Ap Richard became the surname **Pritchard** or **Prichard**. William Prichard was a Welsh exile who settled in Oxford in 1521. Traffic was not always out of Wales into England. A few Englishmen did cross the border to settle or work in Wales, especially around the Cheshire,

Shropshire or Herefordshire borders. The Welsh had a name for them: *sais*, meaning Saxon or Englishman. This led to the surname **Sayce**. Emma Seis lived in Shropshire in 1255 and Jeven Sais in Cheshire in 1392.

The Welsh used the uncomplimentary nickname *Tew* for someone who was fat or plump. The name has remained unchanged to this day as **Tew**. Perhaps Hugh le Tyw, who lived near Chester in 1286, was on the portly side.

The Welsh *gethin* described one who was dusky or swarthy, 'the dark-skinned one'. This led to the surnames **Gething** and **Gittings**. Eynon Gethin lived near Llangollen in 1332. Later, some members of the family moved to Yorkshire; Robert Gettyns was a freeman of York in 1500. *Cynbel* was Welsh for war chief, an unusual nickname as the Welsh were not usually a hostile race. This led to the surname **Kemble**. Robert Kinebald resided in Shropshire in 1215, John Kenebelle was living across England in Suffolk in 1227, while Richard Cembel was an inhabitant of Chirk in 1285.

The Welsh first name Blethyn led to the surnames **Blethyn** and **Pleven**. The first record of the surname was noted in 1173 with Bledienus filius Keneweret who lived near the Shropshire border. Llewellyn Ap Bledyn was mentioned in parliamentary records in 1313. There are at least eight ways of spelling **Prothero**. It stems from the Welsh Ap Riderch, son of *Riderch*, describing someone with a reddish-brown complexion. As late as 1725 the family of Rowland Prythero were still living in Brecon.

Another family name is **Prodgers**, originating from the Welsh Ap Roger. There are two early records of the family living near the Cheshire border, John Ap Rogers, 1538, and Charles Proger, 1607.

One of the few Welsh occupational surnames, **Goff** originated from the Welsh and Breton *gof*, meaning smithy. By 1208 Thomas Goffe had left his native Wales and set up business in Warwick. There are at least eight variations of the surname **Jenkins, Jencken** or **Junkin**. It was first spelt Janekyn, meaning young John. By 1288 the family of Jonkin had moved to Cheshire and in 1296 Richard Janekyn had moved from Wales to Shropshire and then on to Sussex, where he was mentioned in local records.

The surname **Idle** was not given to a lazy ancestor, it sometimes stemmed from the Welsh *ithael*, meaning 'lord bountiful'. Wrennus filius Ydel was living in Hereford in 1193. Two surnames with the same origin are **Ithell** and **Bithell**, from Ap Ithel. Lewlyn Apithell lived in Radnor in 1325. **Jago** came from Iago, the Welsh version of James. William Jeago had left his native Wales to settle in England by 1221. **Welch** or **Welsh** speaks for itself: it was given as a nickname to newcomers who had arrived from Wales. It stemmed from Old English

Welshe. Robert Welch was a citizen of Colchester in 1334. **Probert**, comes from Ap Robert, and **Probin** from Ap Robin. **Maddock** originated from the Welsh *madog*, meaning goodly. Oenus filius Madoc and William Madoc both lived in Wales, but Robert Madduck and his family had moved to England by 1290.

Finally we come to one of the most common surnames in both England and Wales – **Jones**. The Hebrew name was Johanan, the French Johan, and the English John. The Welsh was *Ievan* but the Welsh version used for the Bible was *Ioan*, hence the frequency of Jones in Wales. There have been thousands upon thousands of members of the Jones family over the centuries. One of the first living in Wales was Walterus Jone, mentioned in records in 1279.

Transatlantic surnames

British surnames are found in every part of the English-speaking world, carried there by the settlers and colonisers who made their homes in places as far afield as the United States, Canada, Australia and New Zealand. A large percentage of the inhabitants of the United States are of British origin, starting with the first emigrants who settled in Virginia and those who sailed in the *Mayflower*. Though British surnames have changed in spelling and pronunciation in the last four hundred years, the names that were carried to the North American continent have changed little. In fact, some surnames that have virtually disappeared from Britain are still in use in the United States.

When the *Mayflower* arrived off the coast of New England in 1620, a treaty and code of laws were drawn up before the passengers disembarked. This charter, setting out the internal laws of the new colony, was known as the 'Mayflower Compact' and all the signatures were British surnames. Here, then, are some of these surnames and their history.

The surname **White** must be as common in the United States as it is in Britain. It originated from Old English *hwita*, referring to a man with fair hair or complexion. One of our oldest surnames, it was known in Herefordshire long before the arrival of the Normans. **Warren** on the other hand arrived with the Normans and denoted a man who came from La Varenne in France. Willian de Warene, mentioned in the Domesday Book, held lands in Lincolnshire and Essex, rewards for his services at the Battle of Hastings.

Howland was a pet name for Hugh; the first record of the family comes from Devon with Walter Howlat, resident in the county in 1310. Ralph de Stanedis lived in Standish, Lancashire, in 1206, the birthplace of the surname **Standish**. There were two origins for **Tilley**. Oto de Tilli who lived in York in 1185 could claim descent from followers of William the Conqueror who came from Tilly in France. Simon Tyly, a resident of Sussex in 1296, obtained his surname from old English *tilia*, a farmer or husbandman. **Goodman** stemmed from *godmann*, the master of the house, while **Margeson**, first noted in Suffolk, means the son of Margery. Robert le **Tinker**, who mended pots and pans, lived in Somerset in 1243; this surname was more common in the south.

Many place names contain Ridge, from the Old Norman *hryggr*, and a man who lived in one of these places, or near a ridge, soon attracted the surname **Ridgedale**. Another surname inherited from a place name is **Eaton**, from one of the several Eatons in Berkshire,

Lincolnshire, Norfolk and elsewhere. **Chilton** derived from one of the many places named Chilton but chiefly from the ones in Buckinghamshire, Berkshire, Somerset and Kent. The French term *flechier* described a maker or seller of arrows; one such man was Peter le **Fletcher** who resided in Bedfordshire in 1227.

At first used as a nickname denoting office, and later as a derogatory nickname, **Priest** is one of our oldest surnames; we have a record of an Aelfsige Preost who lived in Hertfordshire in AD 963. *Ceofan* denoted a man who cut in wood or stone; first recorded in Essex, the name is now **Carver**. Brun de **Bradford** lived in Bradford, Yorkshire, hence his surname. From Suffolk we find **Brewster** which in the old days referred to a female brewer, and Yorkshire supplied **Allerton** – son of Allot.

Alden derived from the Anglo-Scandinavian *healfdene* – half Dane. John Alden who lived in Suffolk in 1524 claimed direct descent from an Anglo-Scandinavian family. **Martin** was, and still is, both a Christian name and a surname. It came from Martinus, a forename that stemmed from Mars, the god of war. **Billingham** signified residence in Billingham, Durham or Lincolnshire, or Billing in Northamptonshire.

The Old English for darling was **Mullins**, probably adopted as a surname by a son whose mother possessed this pet name. Among early holders of the name we find William Mulling who lived in the City of London in 1292. **Hopkins** stemmed from the pet name Hobb, rhymed from Rob, short for Robert.

These, then, are just a few of the surnames carried to America by the *Mayflower* in 1620. Within a matter of two or three years, a constant stream of ships sailed across the Atlantic, bearing passengers for the new colony. They took with them surnames from every part of the British Isles, and those surnames are still in use today, completely unchanged in both spelling and pronunciation.

After the arrival of the *Mayflower*, the next most important event in the history of the United States was the War of Independence. From that time on, Americans made their own laws, chose their own governments and instituted the office of President. When the Declaration of Independence was signed in 1776, every signatory possessed a British surname. George **Washington** became the first President; his ancestors came from Washington, near Sunderland, from where they obtained their surname. Ulysses **Grant**, who led the Union forces in the American Civil War, enjoyed two terms as President. His family may have acquired the surname from Old English *grant*, describing a senior or elder member of the family. Abraham **Lincoln**'s family hailed from Lincoln and were mentioned in the Domesday Book. Harry S. **Truman**, the thirty-third President, had the dreadful task of authorising the use of the atom bomb against Japan. His family acquired its name from a nickname which denoted a trustworthy man or one who was faithful. Richard Treweman lived in Kent in 1215.

Warren **Harding**, the twenty-ninth President, had Anglo-Saxon ancestors who had acquired the name from *hearding*, meaning 'the hard one'. James **Madison**, the fourth President, had two origins for his surname, either from the small Scottish village of Maddiston, near Falkirk, or from Old English *madder*, describing a dyer. The name lives on in New York with Madison Gardens and Square. Thomas **Jefferson**, the third President, helped draft the Declaration of Independence and also introduced English landscape gardening into the USA. His name's origins are easy – son of Geoffrey. One ancestor was John Jeffrason, freeman of York in 1528.

Paul **Revere** was the American patriot who rode from Boston to Lexington to warn the revolutionary leaders of the advancing British troops. His ancestors acquired the name from Old English *revere*, meaning robber. By the time William le Revere had acquired the surname in Kent in 1316 it had become respectable. Here are two names from opposing sides of the Civil War: Robert E. **Lee** has many places in the United States named after him. His forebears came from one of the many English places named Lea, Lee or Leigh. General William **Sherman** was his main opponent and towards the end of the war led his army through Georgia. His ancestors came from Suffolk. The name originated from Old English *scearra-mann*, a shearer of woollen cloth. Colonel George **Custer** has gone down in history as the man who was defeated by the combined Indian tribes at Little Bighorn (Custer's Last Stand). His name originated from a maker of feather beds or cushions known as a *courstière*. One such person was Sibilla La Custere who carried on her trade in Somerset in 1254. General George **Patton**, a leading American general in the Second World War, was descended from Hugo Paton, residing in Northumberland in 1230, who acquired the name through the family pet name of Pat for Patrick.

Numerous films portray the nineteenth century as the most romantic era in American history with their colourful representations of Wild West villains and heroes. It was Thomas and Asa **Mercer** who founded the city of Seattle. Their ancestors acquired the surname from the French *mercier*, describing one who dealt in textile fabrics, especially silks, velvets and other expensive materials. One such merchant was Gamel Mercer who carried on his trade in Lincoln in 1168. Davy **Crockett** was a frontiersman and hero who died defending the Alamo against Mexican troops in the struggle for the independence of Texas. His forebears had humble beginnings; the name was derived from Old English *crocca*, meaning a potter. Simon Le Crockere turned his potter's wheel in Oxford in 1279.

Daniel **Boone**, who in the early days of opening up the frontiers explored Kentucky, was another romantic figure. Centuries before, his ancestors lived in Bohon, Normandy, and came over with William the Conqueror; the name is mentioned in the Domesday Book. It was Horace **Greeley** who coined the immortal phrase 'Go west, young man' when he offered this advice in his newspaper, the *New York Tribune*. His ancestors attracted the name from the Old French *greslet*, meaning 'the pock-marked one'. An ancient family, they fought at the Battle of Hastings. Although William **Penn** was an Englishman, he founded the state of Pennsylvania. The name stems from Old English *pen*, meaning hill, for one who dwelt near the hill, or from residence at Penn, Buckinghamshire. Walter de la Penne lived in that village in 1196.

John **Rolfe** was the Englishman who married the Indian princess Pocohontas from Virginia. She visited England, fell ill and died and was buried in Gravesend, Kent. His ancestors were Danes who settled in Lincolnshire; the name means peasant. When the **Chisholm** family left Chisholm in the Scottish Borders to settle in America, little did they know that one of their descendants, Jesse Chisholm, would establish the Chisholm Trail, the famous cattle drive trail from Texas to Abilene.

The old schoolboy hero William **Cody**, better known as Buffalo Bill, started out as a buffalo hunter supplying the men laying the railroad tracks with fresh meat. He went on to establish his Wild West Show which toured the United States and Europe. His forefathers had humble beginnings: the Old English name for a cobbler was *code*, and Nicholas Cody carried on his trade in Warwick in 1250. Born in Texas, Samuel Cody came to England to seek fame and fortune. Interested in aeronautics, he built the first aircraft for the British government in 1908, resulting in the establishment of the Royal Aircraft Establishment at Farnborough.

In the early days Texas was helped by many flamboyant characters. **Dallas** was named after a US Vice President, George Mifflin Dallas. His family originally came from the barony of Dallas in Moray; one member of the family was Henry Dallas who resided in the locality in 1513. **Houston** was named after the politician Samuel Houston who helped Texas join the Union. His ancestors were also Scottish, from the village of Houston in Renfrewshire.

It was Colonel **Dodge** who founded the city that bears his name. Dodge City was the first real frontier town with cowboys, saloons and gunfighters. The surname was derived from the rhyming slang pet name for Roger. It was a far cry from Dodge City to Gloucester, where Nicholas Dodge resided in 1206.

The United States has always been renowned for its inventors and captains of industry. Henry **Ford** invented and developed the mass-produced car. More than fifteen million Model T Fords were sold, his most famous vehicle. His ancestors could have come from almost anywhere in Britain; the name was given to one who lived near a ford or who came from one of the numerous places named Ford. In December 1903 at Kittyhawk, Wilbur and Orvill **Wright** made the first controlled flight in an aeroplane. Some of their ancestors' skills must have rubbed off on them: the surname originated from Old English *wyrhta*, meaning carpenter or joiner.

King Camp **Gillette** was the man who saved his fellow men hours of discomfort when shaving by inventing the modern safety razor. John Gilet, a resident of Durham in 1243, inherited the name from his father, *Guillot*, the French version of William. When Samuel **Slater** arrived in New England in the mid eighteenth century he erected the first thread mill and spinning loom operated by water power. From these humble beginnings grew the vast New England textile factories. Thomas Slater, a roofer or slater, lived in York in 1297 – no doubt his dexterous skills were passed down the generations. Edwin **Land** invented the polaroid camera in 1947. His ancestors acquired the Old English nickname *launde*, describing 'the dweller by the glade'. One of the early holders of the name was James de la Launde who dwelt in Somerset in 1262. The man who probably did more to open up the West than anyone else was Samuel **Morse**, though he did not know it at the time. He experimented with the electric telegraph and invented the now famous code of dots and dashes. Within ten years of his invention an entire network of telegraph lines was set up, linking the whole country. The origins of his ancestors are obscure. The surname was derived from the Latin *mauritius*, meaning the swarthy one.

Apart from his ability as a statesman (he helped draft the Declaration of Independence), Benjamin **Franklin** was a brilliant scientist, one of the pioneers of electricity. His forefathers acquired the Old English nickname *Frankeleyn*, denoting a freeman, a landowner of free – but not noble – birth. Ralph Frankelein, a citizen of York in 1195, cannot have known that one day a descendant of his would help found one of the world's largest democracies.

New York's Fifth Avenue is synonymous with elegant fashion, wealth and affluence. One establishment known world wide for its expensive and exclusive jewellery is **Tiffany**. The name originated from the Latin *Theophania*, an alternative name for Epiphany, usually given to girls born at Epiphany (6th January). Gilbert Tyffayne, who had taken his mother's first name as his surname, was a citizen of York in 1288.

Music, literature and drama have always played an important part in the history of the USA. In the nineteenth century the poems of Walt **Whitman** focused on the American way of life. 'Drum Taps' was about the Civil War. His ancestors acquired their nickname from Old English *hwitmann*, meaning the fair one. One early member of his family was Michael Whitman, living in Colchester in 1310. Walt **Disney** was the father of the animated film industry and head of one of the world's most successful film companies. He could claim that his ancestors arrived in England with William the Conqueror. They took their surname from their place of birth, Isigny in Normandy. One member of the family was William de Ysini, living in Lincoln in 1150.

Nathaniel **Hawthorne** achieved fame as a writer when he wrote *The House of Seven Gables*. His family first lived in Hawthorne, Durham, from where they took their surname. William de Hagethorn was a resident of Durham in 1155. Harriet Beecher **Stowe** caused controversy when she wrote *Uncle Tom's Cabin* in 1852, highlighting the problems of the southern states. Her family was living in England long before the Norman Conquest, taking their name from residence at one of the many places named Stowe. Wulfino de Stowe was mentioned in Anglo-Saxon records of AD 975 in Cornwall.

Mark Twain's books were known to millions but his real name was Samuel **Clemens**. The surname stemmed from the Latin *Clemens*, a nickname meaning mild and merciful. One of his ancestors, Robertus Clemens, was resident in Oxford in 1155. The name Daniel **Emmett** will not mean much to most folk, but the tune 'Dixie' will. He composed the song that became the anthem of the southern states. Emmot was the pet name for Emma, and many men took this, their mother's name, as their surname. Ranulph Emmot, who lived in Warwick in 1332, was probably whistling a tune long before his illustrious descendant dreamt up the now famous song. Stephen **Foster** was also a composer; he penned dozens of songs, such as 'Swanee River', 'My Old Kentucky Home' and the drawing-room ballad 'Jeannie with the Light Brown Hair'. Centuries before, his ancestors had acquired their name from Old English *foster*, describing a nurse or a foster parent. Perhaps John Foster, a citizen of Colchester in 1373, was an adopted child, or his mother may have been a nurse. Long before the Wild West was the subject of films, Zane **Grey** was writing numerous novels about it – some of his later books were used in a few of the early silent films. His surname speaks for itself: it was the nickname given to a grey-haired man. Washington **Irving** was a nineteenth-century writer who first told of Rip Van Winkle. His family was one of many who made their way from Scotland to America; the surname was acquired from their place of birth – Irvine, Ayrshire, or Irving, Dumfries. Victor **Herbert** composed the music for light operas. The nickname *Herbert* derived from the Old Norman meaning 'bright army'. Lastly, the stage surname of Douglas **Fairbanks**, father and son, both film stars, meant the dweller by the fair banks. Robert Fairebank was the son of Richard Farebank, freeman of York in 1583.

Commonwealth surnames

Apart from in the United States, British surnames are still to be found in large numbers in Canada, Australia and New Zealand. The early British pioneers who emigrated to each of these countries had one aim: to find a new home and a better way of life. Today, their descendants are enjoying the fruits of their labours and still bear the same surnames, handed down from one generation to the next.

Emily **Carr** who lived in Victoria, British Columbia, in the early twentieth century was a writer and one of the first 'modern' Canadian painters. Her surname meant the dweller by the marsh or wet ground. John de Car lived in Lancashire in 1332. George **Dawson** was the director of the geological survey during the Klondike gold rush, and Dawson City was named after him. The name means son of Daw, a nickname for David. Roger Daudes resided in Derby in 1372.

Henry **Hind** made one of the first important expeditions into the North West Territories in 1857. His ancestors acquired the nickname for being 'as timid as a deer', something that was certainly not true of himself. John **Molson** acquired fame as the man who built the first Canadian steamboat in 1809. The surname originated from son of Moll, a nickname for Mary. Michael Mollesone resided in Somerset in 1323. Robert **Short** was a naval topographer who in 1759 mapped out Halifax, Nova Scotia. There is no doubt about the origins of his surname, given to one of short stature. It stemmed from Old English *sceort*. One early member of the family was William Short, mentioned in Sussex records in 1327.

Mary **Gallant,** a Canadian novelist, set many of her books in her native city of Montreal. The surname originated from the French *galant*, describing someone who was dashing, or bold or spirited. John Galant was a citizen of Colchester in 1326. Sam **Steele** was in charge of the North West Mounted Police detachment at Dawson City during the Klondike gold rush. He had the job of keeping the peace among twenty thousand gold miners who worked all day and drank and gambled all night. He had the right surname: his name was from Old English *stele*, meaning hard.

William **Bompos** was a Church of England minister who for forty-six years was known as the 'Bishop of the North'. His parish covered thousands of square miles of almost deserted Canadian territory. His was a good choice of surname; it originated from the French *bon pas*, meaning light of foot, or one who could travel at a good pace. Robert **Freeland** was one of the first modern industrialists. In the early 1880s he opened a large soap and candle factory in Toronto. His surname stemmed from Old English *freoland*, indicating a man who held land without obligation, rent or service.

Captain John **Meares** was the first European to obtain land in British Columbia when he set up a trading post in 1788. His ancestors acquired the surname from Old English *mere*, the dweller by the pool. Adam de Mere was a citizen of Wakefield in 1307.

Malcolm **Lowry** was a remittance man. Born into a wealthy family, he was sent out to British Columbia in disgrace to exist on a small pension or remittance. However, he made good and became a well-known and respected writer. The surname stems from son of Laurence; one ancestor was Robert Lowri, living in Cumberland in 1332. Robert **Borden** was Prime Minister of Canada from 1911 to 1920 and through those turbulent years he always insisted on Canada being treated as an independent nation. His ancestors acquired the surname through residence in the village of Borden, Kent. Henry Borden lived in the village in 1317.

John **Simcoe** was named as the first Governor of Upper Canada in 1791. He established his capital at York, which in 1793 was renamed Toronto. His wife Elizabeth kept a diary which contained ninety of her own sketches, accurately reflecting Canadian life as it was then. The surname stems from the nickname Little Sim. One early holder of the family name was Simon Simco, residing in Somerset in 1327.

After Canada the vast lands of Australia were the next to be peopled by Europeans, mostly British. In the first few years the immigrants consisted mainly of convicts, officials, police and military personnel. Free settlers soon followed, however. Sir Thomas **Brisbane**, Governor of New South Wales, sent a surveyor north to explore more of the country. He founded the city of Brisbane (now the capital of Queensland) in 1829. His surname originated from *brise-ban*, meaning 'break bone', a nickname no doubt given to someone of exceptional strength. Ralp Briseban lived in Middlesex in 1275. Still in Queensland, Robert **Towns**, a sea captain, founded the settlement of Townsville. His surname meant the dweller at the end of the village or town.

Point Samson was named in honour of Michael **Samson**, one of the first settlers in Western Australia. Popular in Yorkshire, the surname stemmed from an early Welsh bishop who settled in Brittany. Major Edmond **Lockyer** landed in Western Australia in 1826 and established a military post that later became Albany. His surname was derived from Old English *loc*, describing a locksmith. John Lokyere carried on the trade in Warwick in 1221. Paddy **Hannan** found gold in Kalgoorie, Western Australia, in 1892. At the height of the gold rush the town had twenty-three hotels, six banks and a population of 15,000 (today it numbers less than 1000). His surname was derived from *Hann*, the Flemish version of John. John **Roe** was the first Surveyor General of Western Australia; the town of Roebourns was named after him. The surname stems from the nickname Roe for a man associated with deer, probably a game warden who guarded a forest used for hunting. Isolda Roe resided in Wakefield, Yorkshire, in 1314.

Colonel **Light** founded Adelaide, the first planned Australian city. His surname is derived from Old English *leoht*, the dweller in the glade or clearing. Coffin Bay is named after Sir Issac **Coffin**. The name originated from the maker of coffers – boxes or chests. Thomas le Coffir carried on his trade in London in 1299. The **Henty** brothers founded Portland in 1834, a deep water port and the first penal settlement in Victoria. Their ancestors came from Antye, Sussex, and John de Hentye lived in the village in 1333. James **Esmond** discovered the first gold in Victoria at Clunes in 1851. His ancestors acquired the surname from Old English *Eastmund*, meaning 'favoured by grace' (this happened to be true in his case). Margaret **Catchpole** wrote vivid accounts of life in the penal colony in the early days. A very unusual surname, it originated from the French *cachepol*, meaning 'chase fowl'. The nickname was given to a tax collector who confiscated fowl or poultry in default of money. One such official was Robert Chachepol, resident in Middlesex in 1241. William **Wills** was one of four explorers who made the first south to north crossing of Australia in 1861. On the return journey Wills died of starvation and thirst. It is ironic to think that his surname meant the dweller by the well or springs.

The Australian artist John **Glover** arrived in Tasmania in 1836 and painted many scenes of early life in the colony. The surname is easy: the maker or seller of gloves. William de Glovere carried on his trade in Norfolk in 1250. David **Herbert** was a convict stonemason who in 1836 built the beautiful bridge at Ross, Tasmania, which is still standing today. He received a free pardon in recognition of his labours and became a respected member of the community. The surname came from the Old Norman for 'bright army'; one holder of the name was Christopher Herbert, a freeman of York in 1550.

Captain Walter **Tench** was the marine officer in charge of the first settlement at Sydney Cove. A tench is a fat, freshwater fish, but how a man came to acquire such a nickname has been lost down the centuries. However, William Tenche who lived in Lincoln in 1193 appeared to be quite happy with his name.

David **Berry** founded the New South Wales town bearing his name, built in the early 1820s on the site of a convict settlement. His ancestors acquired the name from Old English *beri*, meaning the servant at the manor house, or the dweller by the enclosure. Little did Hubert Bery, a resident of Bury St Edmunds in 1268, know that one day a descendant of his would help found a new nation.

William **Mills** discovered the site of Alice Springs whilst surveying the route for the overland telegraph line. He named it after the wife of

Charles **Todd**, the Superintendent of Telegraphs for South Australia who built the telegraph line that linked Adelaide with Darwin. Mills meant dweller by the mills; John Myles was a London citizen in 1336. Todd originated from Old English *todde*, meaning a fox. One early holder of the name was Richard Todd who lived in Northumberland in 1231.

New Zealand was the furthest of the British possessions and one of the first to settle in this outpost was Samuel **Leigh** who set up a missionary post in 1821. The origin of his surname reflected his own life in the new country; it meant the dweller by the wood clearing, or derived from residence in one of the many places named Leigh. In 1926 John **Lambert** was the first New Zealand farmer to use an aircraft for crop-dusting. By a strange coincidence his surname originated from the Norman for bright land, introduced from Flanders. No doubt Peter Lambert, a Norfolk farmer living in 1220, used less sophisticated equipment.

The author and farmer Samuel **Butler** owned a huge sheep station called Mesopotamia in the Canterbury district during the second half of the nineteenth century. His ancestors started out as servants rather than masters: the surname stems from the Anglo-French *butuiller*, describing a servant in charge of the wine cellar (not all that different from the job description of a butler). No doubt Henry le Butler, resident in Worcester in 1327, dispensed his master's wine with great care. Joseph **Ward** was Prime Minister of the newly created Dominion of New Zealand in 1907. His ancestors acquired the nickname from Old English *weard*, describing a watchman, the task of William Warde of Ripon in Yorkshire in 1194. Another Prime Minister was John **Ballance**, who introduced a programme of social reform in 1891. His forefathers acquired the name from the French *balancer*, meaning weighing with a balance. Gordon **Coates** was Minister for Public Works in the early 1920s and was responsible for bringing electricity to almost every home, farm and factory in New Zealand. Centuries before, his ancestors came from Cotes in Leicestershire or Staffordshire, or Coates in Wiltshire, Cambridgeshire or Gloucestershire. William de Cotes came from Cotes in Leicestershire in 1290.

Elizabeth **Yates** became the first female mayor in New Zealand in 1893 when she was elected at Onehunga, just after women had won the franchise. Her surname was derived from Old English *geat*, the dweller by the gate. During the dark days of poverty in the early twentieth century Mary **Aubert** nursed the sick and cared for the poor who lived in the Wellington slums. The surname originated from the French *aubert*, meaning noble or bright, truly an accurate description of this lady. One of her ancestors was Isabella Aubert, resident in Suffolk in 1327. Ettie **Route** travelled to Egypt during the First World War to work as a nurse with the New Zealand army. Her main concern was the health and morals of the troops who, thousands of miles from home, faced many temptations. Her surname originated from Old English *rot*, the dweller by the rough ground. Clarice atte Route was a lady of some importance mentioned in Sussex records in 1296. Maud **Basham** was known as Aunt Daisy to thousands of New Zealand housewives. For over twenty years she broadcast a regular morning radio show specifically for women. Her name originated from residence at Barsham in Norfolk or Suffolk, and we have a record of Margaret Bassham of Colchester in 1367.

Conclusion

British surnames did not suddenly appear on the scene in medieval times, to remain unchanged through the centuries. They emerged gradually and, while some are still used in their original form, many have changed considerably over the years, influenced by regional and local dialects and by abbreviated forms of spelling.

The Industrial Revolution introduced a new way of life for millions of people: new trades sprang up; technical terms, hitherto unknown, were used; and new nicknames were compounded. These in time became surnames associated with the steam engine, engineering, steel, gas, and new methods of spinning. All these trades and industries were responsible for new surnames.

Occasionally one comes across a surname for which there seems to be no logical explanation for its origin. It cannot be tracked down to our French, Anglo-Saxon or Scandinavian ancestors, but its modern spelling is the clue that this is a name from the nineteenth century. We have our Victorian forebears to thank for some of these surnames, known as foundling names. Parish beadles and workhouse officials were responsible for many extraordinary and even ridiculous surnames that cannot be traced back to any other known source.

Stealthy footsteps outside the parish workhouse at midnight. The faint whimper of a young child followed by a discreet knock on the door. The parish beadle on investigation finds a baby wrapped in clothes, nestling on the doorstep, the distraught mother already hurried away. Faced with the problem of naming this abandoned child, what better choice than John **Midnight** or **Midwinter**. One poor mite found outside a public institution was found clutching a coin and was named **Halfpenny** by the parish officials. The foundling names of **Monday** and **Friday** speak for themselves, but **Charity** was usually given to a child left in the care of a hospital or church refuge. **Feaveryear**, a country term for February, was the name sometimes given to children abandoned during this cold bleak month. One child found in the streets by a nightwatchman acquired the surname **Waite**, a nickname for a nightwatchman. A few villages or towns had orphanages in early Victorian times, and unknown babies or children left on these premises were given the surnames **Childers**, **Children** or **Childerhouse**, all old-fashioned terms for orphanages.

This coining of new surnames did not cease in the twentieth century, when a large number of political and religious refugees from Europe made new homes in Britain. Many adopted British surnames, perhaps choosing a common surname that sounded similar to their original name, but a few enterprising individuals decided to make up their own surnames. This process is still going on today.

Our surnames are like our way of life, never standing still but continually changing, and offer an intriguing reflection of this constant evolution.

Further reading

Barber, Henry. *British Family Names.* London, 1894 (selected libraries).

Bardsley, C. W. *Dictionary of English and Welsh Surnames.* Heraldry Today, 1901.

Burke's Landed Gentry. Burke's Peerage, 1969.

Cottle, Basil. *The Penguin Dictionary of Surnames.* Penguin, 1994.

Dorwood, D. *Scottish Surnames.* Harper Collins, 2000.

Ekwall, Eilert. *Concise Dictionary of English Place Names.* Oxford University Press, 1989.

Hanks, Patrick, and Hodges, Flavia. *A Dictionary of Surnames.* Oxford University Press, 1998.

International Genealogical Index. Available on microfilm covering all English counties, at most local history libraries.

Reaney, P.H. et al. *A Dictionary of English Surnames.* Oxford University Press, 1997.

Many county and municipal local history libraries possess archives that usually include Poll Tax returns, Subsidy Rolls, Pipe Rolls and local parish records. There are also lists of freemen of various cities throughout England, some dating back to the thirteenth century. These can be inspected, usually by appointment; some of the information may be on microfilm.

The English Place-Name Society has published various works covering most English counties from 1926. A publication giving some technical information on surnames is *Surnames: Genetic Structure* by G. W. Lasker, published by Cambridge University Press, 1985.

Index of surnames

INDEX OF SURNAMES

120